Revelationship

How God Reveals Himself
as He Pursues Us for Relationship

Dr. Randy Colver
Cathy Garland

En Route Books and Media, LLC
Saint Louis, MO

⊕ ENROUTE
Make the time

En Route Books and Media, LLC
5705 Rhodes Avenue
St. Louis, MO 63109

Contact us at **contactus@enroutebooksandmedia.com**

Cover Credit: Tamara Colver Dixon

Copyright 2024 Randy Colver and Cathy Garland

ISBN-13: 979-8-88870-151-5
Library of Congress Control Number: 2024935297

All rights reserved. No part of this book may be reproduced, stored in a retrieval system, or transmitted in any form, or by any means, electronic, mechanical, photocopying, or otherwise, without the prior written permission of the author.

Among the scriptural translations used or consulted were NLT, MSG, NASB, TPT, ISV.

Scripture quotations taken from The Holy Bible, New International Version® NIV® Copyright © 1973, 1978, 1984, 2011 by Biblica, Inc. Used with permission.

Scripture taken from the Holy Bible: International Standard Version® Release 2.0. Copyright © 1996-2013 by the ISV Foundation. Used by permission of Davidson Press, LLC. All rights reserved internationally.

Scripture quotations taken from the (NASB®) New American Standard Bible®, Copyright © 1960, 1971, 1977, 1995, 2020 by The Lockman Foundation. Used by permission. All rights reserved. lockman.org

Scripture quotations marked NLT are taken from the *Holy Bible*, New Living Translation, Copyright © 1996, 2004, 2015 by Tyndale House Foundation. Used by permission of Tyndale House Publishers, Inc., Carol Stream, Illinois 60188. All rights reserved.

THE MESSAGE: The Bible in Contemporary Language. Copyright © 2002 by Eugene H. Peterson. All rights reserved. *THE MESSAGE* Numbered Edition copyright © 2005.

revelationship
/rev·e·la·tion·ship/ • noun

How God reveals himself as he pursues us for relationship

TESTIMONIALS

"This book is a profound challenge to the Body of Christ to wake up to God's passion for a deeper relationship with us. I particularly loved the chapter "The God Who Wrestles With Us." You can always tell when someone has wrestled with God because—like Jacob—they walk differently. The personal stories of Randy and Cathy create a desire in the reader to experience a deeper relationship with God in a fresh transforming experience. This is a must-read!"

– Frank Seamster
Evangelist, https://seamster.org/

"I've known Dr. Randy Colver for over forty years. His life as a husband, a father, a man of God, and a friend is the purest reflection of one who is a mature apprentice (disciple) of Jesus. His daughter Cathy is equally devoted to Christ. They both share an "epignosis" relationship with Jesus. Epignosis simply means an authentic, fully experiential, abiding relationship with Jesus Christ.

Every page of this book will draw you into a transformative encounter with the Lord. "Revelationship" is a precursor of revival where the Word marries the Spirit."

– Elder Yul Crawford
Atlanta Metropolitan Cathedral

"The concept of this book is absolutely ingenious and so necessary. What a gift this resource will be to the body of Christ!"

– Larry Sparks, MDiv.
Publisher, Destiny Image
Author, Pentecostal Fire
LarrySparksMinistries.com

"The writers have poured you a glass of hope, for you hold an insightful and valuable book in your hand. Randy and Cathy offer you an open door through which you are welcome to come in and drink deeply of the Lord's presence. There you will be surprised, enlarged, and instructed by God on what the love and fear of God really means, which is to know him through his word and the revelation of his presence."

– Nita G Berquist
Bible Teacher and Author
Kent, Washington

"Dr. Colver and his daughter, Cathy, take you into a deeper understanding of the nature of God and his pursuit of us. They create a ladder of experiences through each chapter based on their personal encounters with God that will stimulate a greater hunger to know him and pursue Him. It is truly transformational and the questions, devotional readings, and time of reflection and prayer in the companion devotional guide drive home a deeper, applicable experience in your own journey in Christ. I highly recommend any book whose authors know God and provoke me to grow. This clearly is one of those books."

– Dr. Jay Zinn
Founder and Author,
DiscipleshipGroup.com

"Revelationship is more than a book. It is a God-encounter…the Bible verse, 'Taste and see that the Lord is good' (Psalms 34: 8, NIV), becomes alive and tangible. Revelationship is a tool in the hands of Jesus for Christians to know him and be known by him. This is an experience I won't soon forget, leaving me longing for the next chapter and more of Him."

– Sharon Mullins
Pastor of Coweta Community Church
cccnewnan.org

"A powerful message that speaks to every Christian of how the transformative activity of God in our lives draws us ever closer to him."

– Dr. Sebastian Mahfood, OP
Founder and President, WCAT Radio

"If you are pursuing to create or deepen a personal relationship with God, then read this book. Why? The authors cite example after example of biblical passages which specifically highlight why God desires to reveal Himself on a personal and intimate level. Each chapter is filled with not only insights from Scripture, but also personal experiences from their own lives of how revelationship transformed and deepened their understanding of God's love and goodness. So, if you're looking for practical and thoughtful insights having a revelationship with God, then you will not be disappointed."

– Dr. Alan Cureton
Former President
Northeastern University – St. Paul

TABLE OF CONTENTS

Testimonials iiii

Foreword xi

Introduction by Randy 1

Introduction by Cathy 8

Chapter One: "Where are you?" 15

Chapter Two: Revelationship through Scripture 25

Chapter Three: The God Who Hides from Us 39

Chapter Four: The God Who Dwells among Us 47

Chapter Five: The God Who Wrestles with Us 63

Chapter Six: The God Who Rescues Us 73

Chapter Seven: The God Who Disturbs Us 83

Chapter Eight: Revelationship through Prayer and the God Who Heals Us 92

Chapter Nine: The God Who Whispers to the Hurting 103

Chapter Ten: Revelationship in Nature 112

Chapter Eleven: Revelationship through Covenant 125

Chapter Twelve: Revelationship through Suffering and
    the God Who Wants Our Whole Life 135

Chapter Thirteen: Revelationship through History 143

Chapter Fourteen: Revelationship through Church 158

Chapter Fifteen: A Lifetime of Revelationship 168

A Final Word: Responding in Revelationship 177

FOREWORD

I heard it said that God's first language is not English. Nor is it Hebrew or Greek, for that matter. God communicates and engages with his people in so many unique ways because he is a Father, not a formula.

In leading and ministering at revival gatherings around the world, one thing I've come to discover is that God touches each person personally and uniquely.

This book truly brings a much needed and a revelatory "Ah-ha" to countless believers who often feel spiritually inferior or inadequate because they did not experience God in one particular or sensational way.

Revelationship removes the veil of spiritual confusion and encourages all believers that God is a relational Father who communicates, interacts, and meets with his people in so many unique ways. They are all profoundly Biblical, and furthermore, will never contradict or contrast the character of God as revealed through Scripture.

This book will open your eyes and ears to the amazing, supernatural, and relational ways that God is already moving in your life!

Larry Sparks, MDiv.
Publisher, Destiny Image
Author, *Pentecostal Fire*
larrysparksministries.com

INTRODUCTION BY RANDY

Call to me and I will answer you and tell you great and unsearchable things you do not know.
—Jeremiah 33:3 (NIV)

Athanasius, the fourth-century defender of the deity of Christ against the Arians, once posed the question, "Why did God make them [humanity] at all if he did not wish to be known by them?" As a young man, he was writing a treatise called *On the Incarnation of the Word*, which caught the attention of the church authorities in Alexandria, Egypt. Athanasius understood what we often forget: that God desires to relate to humankind by revealing himself—that Christianity is thoroughly about relationship with our Creator. And that deepening our *relationship* with him means having deeper *revelations* of him.

Jesus once said, in a sort of mild rebuke to his disciple Philip, "Don't you know me, Phillip, even after I have been among you such a long time? Anyone who has seen me has seen the Father" (John 14:9, NIV). The incarnation—where God took on human flesh to reveal himself—remains the pinnacle of God's revelation of his nature and Person. As a result, Christianity is "incurably irreverent,"[1] in the words of C. S. Lewis because the God of the universe came to us not in a palace but in a dirty animal stall. He revealed himself in the raw, earthly way we can understand. He came to us as Jesus (the) Christ of Nazareth, God's unique Word—or divine revelation.

> This is "revelation-ship." When he reveals himself, our relationship with him deepens. When our relationship deepens, he reveals himself further—on and on, deeper and further, in grace-filled and Spirit-filled interaction until Christ is also revealed through us.

---

[1] C.S. Lewis, *Introduction*, in J. B. Phillips, *Letters to Young Churches: A Translation of the New Testament Epistles* (New York: Macmillan), viii.

So, he came. And we have seen him, touched him, heard him, as his disciple John said (1 John 1:1). And we rejected him, beat him, spit on him, and drove nails into his hands and feet. Still, he came—weeping over Jerusalem even though they would soon hang him on a cross—washing and wiping the feet of the disciples, even the feet of the one who would soon betray him—forgiving us even in the agonies of death. At each turning point, he revealed the Father's heart.

This is "revelationship." When he reveals himself, our relationship with him deepens. When our relationship deepens, he reveals himself further—on and on, deeper and further, in grace-filled and Spirit-filled interaction until Christ is also revealed through us.

"That I might know him" was the great yearning of the apostle Paul, the persecutor-turned-disciple of Jesus. But our Lord had to first introduce himself in such a way that he could break through the religious stubbornness of Saul the Pharisee. That meant blinding him, knocking him off his horse, and speaking audibly to him. The Messiah revealed himself to Saul, and he was never the same.

Paul abruptly came to understand what Jesus meant when he said, "Now this is eternal life: that they may know you, the only true God, and Jesus Christ, whom you have sent" (John 17:3, NIV). Eternal life is all about relationship. Where we might expect a theological explanation for eternal life, Jesus instead uses relational terms—what we call in this book "revelationship." Eternal life *is* a personal relationship with the Messiah. And the revelation of Jesus on that road to Damascus inaugurated Paul's relationship with the true Lord.

It doesn't stop at the dawning of a relationship, though. Revelationship with God is an eternal thing—ever deepening in wondrous revelations of his character—ever broadening in the awareness of his creative works—ever filling us with his gracious love.

This book, then, is about revelationship—about relationship with the Father through the Son by the power of the Spirit—about relationship through revelation, and revelation through relationship. Revelation comes in unique and varied ways, and we will examine several of these. But as we begin, let us agree with Francis Schaeffer, who observed, "He is there—and he is not silent."

Download our accompanying Devotional Study Guide for FREE at Revelationship.net. It contains mindful study questions, devotional cues, and journaling prompts to help you as chronicle God's revelations to you as he pursues you for a deeper relationship.

FREE DOWNLOAD!
DEVOTIONAL GUIDE & WORKBOOK

REVELATIONSHIP.NET

INTRODUCTION BY CATHY

Even though I am from the wrong generation entirely, I owe much of my spiritual life to the hippies who became radically saved in the Jesus movement. My mother received salvation on a commune during the height of the hippie movement and became a radically saved Jesus Freak (complete with the fringed Jesus Freak purse). My father received salvation in the Methodist Church he attended as a teenager and then received the baptism of the Holy Spirit during the Jesus Movement. My father's passion for the scriptures was obvious and he quickly became an ordained Teacher and Pastor.

Because of their dedication to the Body of Christ, I have abundant memories of sleeping underneath pews on faded, orange carpet and spending hours at church, learning to love God's people. So, when I say "I sat under" godly men and women who taught the

Word of God to the newly saved hippies, I mean it literally and figuratively.

Growing up in the church may place one at risk of becoming wounded by others in the church—and I know many who have scars from the treatment they suffered at the hands of church authorities. I experienced some of that wounding, but I was mostly protected by the buffer of our family circle, which included my grandmother, cousins, aunts, and uncles. In our family circle, it was common to constantly talk about God, the Bible, what God was saying to the church, prayer, revival…these things were always on our mind, and we talked of them constantly. *Revival was at the top of our priorities.*

When I turned 13, I rebelled. I told my parents that I wasn't sure that Christianity was for me. Instead of panicking, my father took me to the library.

Introduction by Cathy

Together, we checked out a stack of books on different religions that was about as tall as I was. It was very easy to eliminate several religions immediately. (For example, I had no intention of subjugating myself to a Muslim man or having my right to drive taken away from me, so the Muslim religion was an easy one to eliminate!)

Other religions were a little bit more difficult to pierce, but by the end of my 13th year I realized that Christ was who he said he was and that I had been created by a Creator to glorify him. I could either accept that purpose or reject it and him entirely. I re-dedicated my life to the Lord and never looked back.

> I *love* the theology and the Word of God. I love to talk about both with anyone who will tolerate me.

Later, after a heart-breaking divorce in my twenties and other disappointments, I found a book called *Absolute Surrender* by Andrew Murray. It was tucked between some other 1960-1970's pea-soup green books in my grandmother's bookcase. When I read *Absolute Surrender,* I knew that I had finally found the source of power that would keep my spiritual life from the lows and highs that had plagued it. (You know what I mean. We go high when we go away to revival at a Youth Summer Camp and then low when we fail to live it on our own.) It was something that many of my fellow young adults often discussed. But I had found the power-source—*surrender*—that has kept me hotly pursuing God's transformative presence for these past two decades.

I *love* the theology and the Word of God. I love to talk about both with anyone who will tolerate me.

Luckily, my family shares in this obsession. In one of our many discussions, Dad and I began to talk about a way to study that the Holy Spirit showed me. This new way made the Old Testament come alive. The Old Testament was no longer a dry and dusty read but, instead, transformative. It had come through a prompting by the Holy Spirit to remember a very important lesson from C. S. Lewis' *The Lion, the Witch, and the Wardrobe* series: look for Aslan. Of course, in *The Lion, the Witch, and the Wardrobe*, Aslan represents Christ. So, as I read the Old Testament looking for the revelation of Christ, what had once seemed ancient, irrelevant—even bloody and legalistic—was transformed. Genesis, Exodus, Leviticus, Deuteronomy, and even Numbers all came together in the revelation of the eternal Christ.

As I shared my new-found passion for the Old Testament, Dad invited me to speak to his group of interns at his church. It was with these same interns that Dad was talking about revelation and how revelation is necessary for relationship, that he accidentally wrote the word *Revelationship* on the board. *Aha!* The rest is history. Or, rather, the rest is written in this book.

Journal Prompt: How has Jesus Christ broken through to reveal himself as the solution to one of your specific needs or lack?

Download our accompanying Devotional Study Guide for FREE at Revelationship.net. It contains mindful study questions, devotional cues, and journaling prompts to help you as chronicle God's revelations to you as he pursues you for a deeper relationship.

CHAPTER ONE

"WHERE ARE YOU?"

My people are being destroyed because they don't know me.

—Hosea 4:6 (NLT)

Have you ever had the feeling that something is missing—especially during those rare pauses in the day or even rarer contemplative moments? For Christians, the feeling is probably the gentle prompting of the Holy Spirit reminding us that we are neglecting our relationship with our Lord. It lies behind the first question God raised to Adam and Eve after they had fallen into sin: *"Where are you?"*

Now, this question doesn't mean that God couldn't find Adam and Eve. On the contrary, he knew exactly where they were. The question derives not from God's omnipresence or omniscience, but from his immanence (present-ness). Due to their rebellion against God's command to them, Adam and Eve's relationship with God was broken. They sensed this and were hiding from God's presence. He called out to them so they would recognize the depth of their separation.

Can you feel God's heartbreak over the rift? The thought of God walking alone in the garden where they previously walked together may be one of the most heartbreaking events in the whole of the Bible.

In this passage and elsewhere in the Bible, God reveals to us that he is both transcendent and immanent. He is not some divine clockmaker who wound up the universe and set it off on its way until it eventually winds down with a gasp and a whimper. He is, in fact, deeply committed and concerned about our lives. Despite his complete "otherness," he wants to be *known*.

> We desperately need God's presence—not just his omnipresence, but his immanent presence. He is there to support us, to prompt us in the way we should go. In the simple and hard things of everyday life, his still, small voice speaks to us. And when we are in communion with him—practicing his presence — our relationship deepens daily.

"Where are you?" He still asks us that today—in the busy chores and family responsibilities, in the day-to-day challenges at work, in the ever-demanding pull of entertainment. We dismiss that nagging feeling that something is missing. Something deep within our souls lacks fulfillment. Something that was meant to be a primary part of us—our relationship with our Creator—has instead been squeezed into an hour on Sunday, forced out by an overflowing To Do List, or maybe remembered a few moments before we fall asleep.

We desperately need God's presence—not just his omnipresence, but his immanent presence. He is there to support us and prompt us in the way we should go. In the simple and hard things of everyday life, his still, small voice speaks to us. And when we are in communion with him—practicing his presence—our relationship deepens daily.

For some, however, like Moses, the yearning for relationship with God becomes the major pursuit of life. Following the Exodus of the Israelites from Egypt, Moses asked God to "teach me your ways so I may know you and continue to find favor with you" (Exodus 33:13, NIV). God responded with a promise that his presence would go with Moses and that he would bring the Israelites into rest.

But also notice how Moses' revelationship did not stop with the initial promise. Moses' pursuit of God's presence led him to request that God reveal his glory. We cannot miss what F. F. Bruce pointed out regarding this: when God passed by to reveal his glory to Moses, *he declared his goodness.* There is a close connection between God's glory and the revelation of his character—of which his goodness is an essential part. To know God in deeper ways means to understand his character more and more. God desires to fill the earth with his glory, and that means revealing his character.

This shows us how revelationship works. God revealed himself to Moses and the relationship was deepened. Then, because of the relationship, Moses asked for further revelation.

God greatly desires revelationship. Where we might expect God to describe the Exodus only in terms of leading the people of Israel to the Promised Land, he instead describes it in relational terms: "I carried you on eagles' wings and brought you *to myself*" (Exodus 19:24, NIV). In a similar way, when Jesus prays about leaving the disciples soon for heaven, he describes it in relational terms: "I want those you have given me *to be with me* where I am and to see my glory" (John 17:24, NIV).

When we turn a few pages of the Bible beyond the Exodus to the story of Gideon, we find another clear example of revelationship. During Gideon's lifetime, the Israelites were in the Promised Land, but found themselves oppressed by the raiding Midianites. Gideon was threshing wheat in a winepress to hide it from the raiders when the angel of the Lord appeared to him and called him a mighty warrior—rather ironic considering the circumstances. (Can you just see Gideon looking around wondering who the angel is referring to?)

The angel promised Gideon his support to defeat the Midianites and thereby bring peace. Through all this, Gideon had a revelation of God as Yahweh-Shalom, meaning, "the Lord is our peace." Through several consecutive tests, God not only revealed himself to Gideon and to Israel, but also revealed who Gideon could be through God's grace. Over time, Gideon became that mighty warrior God foretold.

God sovereignly revealed himself to Gideon through the revelation of his name (the Lord our

Peace) and thereby revealed his nature to meet the deepest need of an oppressed nation. Gideon then asked for further revelation when he laid out each fleece. As a result of this revelationship, Gideon learned to trust God. Revelationship brought an understanding of the faithfulness of God for the coming deliverance, so Gideon learned to walk in unquestioning obedience to God.

We should also notice that, as with both Moses and Gideon, sometimes God reveals himself through angels. Several generations of my family have had angels appear in person and in dreams. In one such dream, I (Randy) was standing on the porch looking out toward the woods at night. God showed me demonic spirits on the edge of these woods who were mocking me. Suddenly, they grew quiet, and a look of dire concern crossed their faces. I turned and looked over my right shoulder to see what they were looking at. Just over my shoulder stood a large, mighty angel staring at the demons. In this revelation, God was showing me that his power and authority were present—though often unseen—to provide protection.

When God meets our needs, he often reveals something about his character. To Moses and Gideon, it was that God establishes peace through victory over their enemies. To Randy, it was a reminder that he could rest in the protection of God against demonic forces. Through them all, revelationship with God deepened.

Of course, when we look to the New Testament, we know that God revealed the deepest part of his nature through the death, burial, and resurrection of Jesus Christ. He did this so that we might know the Father and the Son and thus obtain eternal life—eternal relationship with God in his presence (John 17:3).

God's desire and plan has always been to restore the intimate relationship broken by Adam and Eve in the Garden, answering once and for all the haunting question, "Where are you?"

Journal Prompt: Have you ever felt you were hiding from God? What lengths did God go through to restore you to his presence?

Download our accompanying Devotional Study Guide for FREE at Revelationship.net. It contains mindful study questions, devotional cues, and journaling prompts to help you as chronicle God's revelations to you as he pursues you for a deeper relationship.

CHAPTER TWO

REVELATIONSHIP THROUGH SCRIPTURE

You study the Scriptures diligently because you think that in them you have eternal life. These are the very Scriptures that testify about me...

—John 5:39 (NIV)

A young teacher stands in the synagogue to read from the Isaiah scroll.

"The Spirit of the Lord is on me, because he has anointed me to preach good news to the poor. He has sent me to proclaim freedom for the prisoners and recovery of sight for the blind, to release the oppressed, to proclaim the year of the Lord's favor" (Luke 4:18–19, NIV).

Stopping there, he returns the scroll to the attendant and sits down.

It is one of those moments when all the attention in the world seems fixed on the words to be spoken next. Does this rabbi know when the Messiah will appear? Is the time of deliverance from the Roman oppressors at hand? Is this the year of the Lord's favor? Why didn't this rabbi read the remaining portion about the "day of vengeance"?

Then he speaks. "Today this scripture is fulfilled in your hearing."

Jesus directs their attention to himself. He talks of revelationship through Scripture: all prophets, like Elijah, are rejected by their own. The markers are there, pointing to Jesus—to the salvation he offers—but not all will receive him.

They would rather throw him off a cliff.

The Scriptures are, of course, the most essential and reliable way God reveals himself to us. This is not to rule out God's voice speaking to us through supernatural ways, such as by angels, during prayer, and by the gifts of the Spirit, etc. But the Bible provides revelation that leads us to salvation, shows us how to live godly lives, and remains the standard by which to measure other Spirit-led revelations that we may receive. The apostle Paul confirmed this when he described all Scripture as inspired by God and profitable for godly living (2 Timothy 3:16, NIV).

Studying and reading the Bible is, therefore, essential to knowing God better. There is no shortcut to understanding its meaning and, therefore, studying it diligently is essential. But we should also read the Bible devotionally, as a lover of the Lord who reveals himself in Scripture. We should read it in such a way that we encounter him. Coming to the Bible this way means we come with open hearts—that we aren't just students of the Word, but that we desire to come "face to face with the living God" and walk with him in intimacy.

This is often "...where we walk with the God who is surprising, dangerous, mysterious, alongside us though we fail to recognize Him, then disappearing the minute we do."[2]

If you read the Bible quickly, it will benefit you only a little. Instead, as the devotional writer Madame Guyon wrote, "Plunge into the very depths of

---

[2] Mark Buchanan, *The Holy Wild: Trusting in the Character of God* (Sisters, Oregon: Multnomah Publishers, 2003), 23.

the words you read until revelation, like a sweet aroma, breaks out upon you." Pause as you read to allow the scriptures to gently turn your mind away from distractions and onto Christ. Read scriptures purposely, forming a prayer from your heart. As you draw near to him, he draws near to you, so you may be nourished by the bread of his Word and transformed by his presence.

Along these lines, we can open the revelations of Scripture by personalizing its promises. For instance, the first chapter of Ephesians contains several well-known promises we can appropriate, and which are themselves directed toward revelationship: "I keep asking that the God of our Lord Jesus Christ, the glorious Father, may give you the Spirit of wisdom and revelation, so that you may know him better. I pray also that the eyes of your heart may be enlightened in order that you may know the hope to which he has called you, the riches of his glorious inheritance in the saints, and his incomparably great power for us who believe" (Ephesians 1:17–19, NIV).

I (Cathy), often declare these verses over my children at night while they sleep, substituting the pronouns with their names. As we ask God to reveal these promises to us personally, revelationship is deepened.

As a mother, I'm also facilitating a budding revelationship between my own children and Christ. Recently, my three-and-a-half-year-old daughter—who has sung herself to sleep all her life and never struggled to fall asleep—suddenly became afraid of going to sleep in her room. She had a nightlight, and she had no reason to be afraid, but the first night she got up 15 times. The second night, 20 times.

The third night, we realized we had to equip her to face her fears. We did so by having her declare over herself one of the many scriptures she's memorized: "Be strong and courageous, do not be afraid for the

Lord your God will be with you wherever you go" (Joshua 1:9, NIV). The next night, through her hysterics, she called out to God, "I am strong and courageous!" and "God is with me!" and "God help me!" And he did. She fell asleep right after the worst of the struggle. In the morning, she told me that she saw Jesus and several angels. She said Jesus was so big he filled her room and that his angels were outside the windows blocking them with their wings. These fears did not return.

Scripture is "sharp as a surgeon's scalpel" (Hebrews 4:12, MSG), to put it in the paraphrased words of Eugene Peterson in his Message Bible. But has the Bible become dull and blunted to us? Unfortunately, for many Christians today, the Bible is just one book among many others on the bedside table.

Even those who read it more frequently often use the same translation so many times that their minds wander as they read. The "transporting or horrifying realities of which the book tells may come to us blunted and disarmed and we may only sigh with tranquil veneration when we ought to be burning with shame or struck dumb with terror or carried out of ourselves by ravishing hopes and adorations" to quote C. S. Lewis. "The real sanctity, the real beauty and sublimity of the New Testament (as of Christ's

> We should, of course, come to the Scriptures also as a student, as a disciple to learn at the master's feet. But sometimes we should come to wash his feet with our tears. In deep conviction and repentance—in mourning for our sins—we are captivated by his love that reached for us while we were still sinners. *Revelationship is courtship, too.*

life) are of a different sort: miles deeper and *further in*." ³

The Bible wasn't dull and boring on the road to Emmaus when the disciple's hearts "burned within them" while Christ explained the Scriptures (Luke 24:25-27, 30-32). When was the last time our hearts "burned" within us as we read the Bible? When was the last time we came to the Bible to be changed? When was the last time we encountered the Christ of Scripture as a lover?

We should, of course, come to the Scriptures also as a student, as a disciple to learn at the Master's feet. But sometimes we should come to wash his feet with our tears. In deep conviction and repentance—in mourning for our sins—we are captivated by his love

---

³ C.S. Lewis, *Introduction*, in J. B. Phillips, *Letters to Young Churches: A Translation of the New Testament Epistles* (New York: Macmillan) viii.

that reached for us while we were still sinners. *Revelationship is courtship, too.*

Have you experienced the Passionate Shepherd as he woos you with his love, offering himself as your provider and lover, inviting you to prove his faithfulness?

Scripture "becomes holy ground on which we meet with God and consummate our love for him. It is wonderful, mysterious and beautiful," as Chris Webb put it, "just like its wonderful, mysterious and beautiful Inspirer."[4]

Revelationship also means using our imagination to place ourselves in that synagogue with that young rabbi, Jesus, listening as he read from the scroll. It means placing ourselves in the boat with Peter and the other disciples as we hear how Jesus commanded

---

[4] Chris Webb, *Fire of the Word*, 53.

them to put out a little from the shore and cast their nets.

Do you sense the reluctance of the professional fishermen to obey the words of a carpenter, just as we are often reluctant to obey his words today? Nevertheless, something in the way the Lord spoke or looked—the author doesn't tell us—caused them to finally obey. (What way is he looking into our lives and speaking to us? In what area are we reluctant to obey him?)

What a blessing came about by their obedience! Can you see them frantically trying to pull in the overwhelming catch of fish—more than two boatloads? (What blessing does God want to pour into our lives if we obey him?)

That's when the realization comes over Peter: he is in the presence of the Messiah—for only the Messiah could do such a miracle. A profound sense of shame and conviction strikes him to his core—I am a sinner in the presence of a holy man! He drops his nets and worships at the feet of Jesus.

Through a sanctified imagination, we can put ourselves in Peter's place so that some of his revelation of Christ becomes part of our relationship with him as well. The authors of the Bible intended for their readers to share the wonders of their relationship with the Lord to deepen our relationship. They have walked before us and have so much to share.

I (Randy) have also been personally enriched by certain expositions of Scripture. Scripture contains many propositions to live by, as well as revelations of the Persons of the Trinity, and we can benefit through the preaching and teaching of these truths. In one case, when I was in Bible school, I ran across an interesting title of a scholarly article in a lexicon. At the time you couldn't find such articles online—that was very limited—so I ordered it by interlibrary loan.

The article arrived after several days, and I excitedly tore open the package. To my disappointment, the article assumed readers would know four or five languages. Nevertheless, I persisted through the English parts and managed to get the gist of the meaning. Then, in the summary it all came together, and I understood what the author was saying. To this day, this deeper study has brought me one of the deepest revelations of Jesus and his supremacy that I have ever read.

Journal Prompt: How do you make room in your life for meditation on specific passages to allow the Holy Spirit to transform you?

Download our accompanying Devotional Study Guide for FREE at Revelationship.net. It contains mindful study questions, devotional cues, and journaling prompts to help you as chronicle God's revelations to you as he pursues you for a deeper relationship.

FREE DOWNLOAD!
DEVOTIONAL GUIDE & WORKBOOK
REVELATIONSHIP.NET

CHAPTER THREE

THE GOD WHO HIDES FROM US

God did this so that they would seek him and perhaps reach out for him and find him, though he is not far from any one of us.

—Acts 17:27 (NIV)

I (Cathy) love to play hide and seek with my toddlers because I love their squeals of joy when they find me. I hide just enough to make the adventure of searching worthwhile. They find me hiding behind the drapes but with my toes showing, or in the laundry basket with a hat on my head. The laughter and shouts of "I found you! I found you!" accompanies their attempt to climb in the basket for their turn for me to "find" them in the same spot.

Just as I hide from my toddlers, God often hides himself from us so we can experience the thrill of finding him—discovering him through revela-tionship. He hides himself in the folds and bends of the path of our

> Discovering God endures as one of our great missions in life. Having found him, we are called to remain in him, abiding in his presence. This transforms us, equipping and commissioning us to bring glory to God. We thus fulfill our purpose: *to reveal God's glory through our own story*.

life, taking different roles in our stories—suddenly appearing as the Rescuer, disappearing again only to reveal himself as the Beloved who knows us better than we know ourselves. Our stories and the revelations of him prove to us that the God who created us is the God who wants to be found.

Oh, the joy in the finding!

Discovering God endures as one of our great missions in life. Having found him, we are called to remain in him, abiding in his presence. This transforms us, equipping and commissioning us to bring glory to God. We thus fulfill our purpose: *to reveal God's glory through our own story.*

Since each person's story is unique, there are almost limitless ways to display God's glory. Every time God reveals himself, our story gleams with a new and brilliant facet of his glory—a facet never displayed before and never displayed the same again.

Many times, this glory is displayed when God meets our needs. A perfect example of this is when Jesus performed his first miracle in Cana of Galilee, turning water to wine and rescuing the wedding party, thus revealing his glory (John 2:11).

Once, when our family was much younger and we had little income, my mother (Cathy's paternal grandmother) came to visit. While there, she noticed that we had very few groceries in our kitchen cupboards. She decided it was time to change that, so she gathered us to pray. (Now, you need to understand: My mother was a prayer warrior, and she didn't pray a short, "if you can" kind of prayer. This is your "In the name of Jesus, we command the provision of God" kind of prayer. The kind that sends chills down your spine.) Ten minutes later, the mail arrived, and an unexpected check for several hundred dollars sent the week before by our family in Alaska. (Yes, we had a great trip to the grocery store.) To us, the glory of God visited our home that day.

George Mueller's story is a perfect example of this as well. He founded and directed several orphan houses in the mid-1800s in Bristol, England, and received a revelation from God through a singular verse of Scripture: "Fear the Lord, you his saints, for those who fear him lack nothing" (Psalm 34:9, NIV). Based on this, Mueller determined to ask God alone to meet the needs of the orphans. "To the glory of the Lord, whose I am, and whom I serve, I would state again that every shilling of this money, and all the articles of clothing and furniture, which have been mentioned in the foregoing pages, have been given to me, without one single individual having been asked by me for anything."[5]

---

[5] George Muller, *A Narrative of Some of the Lord's Dealings with George Muller* (London: J. Nisbet & Co., 1855), 187.

Mueller's autobiography tells of years of faithful provision the Lord sent to support the orphans—miracle provision after miracle provision—by his prayers alone. Practical provision came, such as a milk truck that broke down on their doorstep when they had nothing with which to feed the children. God revealed himself as the God who provides, and Mueller (and all the orphans) were never the same.

Story after story in the Bible demonstrates a God who, though hidden, can be found—who, though mysterious, can suddenly be luminous. Just as the Beloved in the Song of Solomon hides momentarily among the clefts of the rock, so our hearts burst for him when we see his penetrating gaze through the lattice—drawing us after him with his satisfying presence.

In Genesis alone, we find the God who, for Adam and Eve, is the God who calls out of the darkness of sin and separation. For Cain, we find the God who shows mercy even in our sin. For Noah, we find the God who grieves for us and contends for us, even in our sin. (Noah's story also reveals the God who provides hope and makes a way of salvation for sinners.) For Abraham, we find the God who comes down to earth to see the sin of humankind, yet credits faith as righteousness. For Lot and Hagar, we find the God who sees injustice and rescues us. And on and on.

Once you start on the quest for the God who hides himself, it will change you because *you will find him* (Jeremiah 29:13 and Isaiah 55:6). He leaves just enough of himself in view that you can discover more of him. At each discovery, you may be "surprised by joy" as C. S. Lewis was, or "undone" like Isaiah, or blissfully set free like Martin Luther, but you are guaranteed to find revelationship.

Journal Prompt: Has God revealed himself to you in unexpected ways? Where have you found God that was least expected?

Download our accompanying Devotional Study Guide for FREE at Revelationship.net. It contains mindful study questions, devotional cues, and journaling prompts to help you as chronicle God's revelations to you as he pursues you for a deeper relationship.

CHAPTER FOUR

THE GOD WHO DWELLS AMONG US

My dwelling place also will be with them; and I will be their God, and they will be my people.
—Ezekiel 27:37 (NASB)

Imagine a goat herder settling down by his evening fire on the mountain slopes of the Sinai desert during the time of the journey of the nation of Israel to the Promised Land. As he stirs the fire he built, he looks up and notices that the mountainside is glowing—but not from his little fire. Peering around a boulder, he looks down into the valley and sees the most incredible sight. There below him, spread out in the valley, is the entire encampment of Israelites! And in the middle of the camp lies a tent structure above which burns an immense flame—lighting the entire valley. He thinks to himself, "What amazing thing is this? That fire can only be the presence of God."

Ch. 4: The God Who Dwells among Us

Since the very beginning, God has desired to dwell among us—and thus make himself known to us. So much did he desire this, that he handpicked a group of people, the Israelites, to demonstrate his glory to the rest of the world. After bringing them out of slavery in Egypt by "his mighty hand," he placed a pillar of cloud over them by day and a pillar of fire by night. When either moved, the camp broke and followed God's presence wherever it would lead.

God commanded the Israelites to build a temporary residing place for his presence—the tent, or

> The Bible also shows that, after his resurrection and ascension, Jesus sent the Holy Spirit into the hearts of believers, making us now—individually and collectively—the temple of God's presence. The light that once made the mountains glow now penetrates hearts. God had moved into an entirely new level of revelationship with his people—indwelling them by the Holy Spirit.

tabernacle—where he met with the Israelites and "ate" with them in symbolic fellowship through the ritual sacrifices. At this "table of the Lord," life was spilled out by the blood of the sacrifices to provide temporary atonement for sin so that fellowship could ensue with a holy God. It is above this tabernacle that his glory overshadowed his people and within its structure that his actual presence—the Shekinah—dwelt like a footstool for his throne in heaven.

It was here, at the tent of his presence, that God met with the people and gave Moses direction. The first result, then, of God's "indwelling the nation" was that they had a direct and intimate way to communicate with him.

The Bible also shows that, after his resurrection and ascension, Jesus sent the Holy Spirit into the hearts of believers, making us now—individually and collectively—the temple of God's presence. The light that once made the mountains glow now penetrates hearts. God moved into an entirely new level of revelationship with his people—indwelling them by the Holy Spirit.

It follows also that God made a new way to reveal himself to us. Jesus confirmed this when he said that the Spirit will take from what is his and make it known to us (John 16:13-15). While we often relate this to prayer, we should not overlook the gifts of the Spirit as part of this revelationship. In fact, the *charismata* play a vital role in connecting us to Christ's current, active ministry in heaven. And while we often focus on the gifts of the Spirit for supernatural healings and miracles, several of the gifts fit into God's method of communication with us, particularly words of knowledge and wisdom, discerning of spirits, prophecy, and even, with interpretation, speaking in tongues. Of course, all the gifts help in different ways to deepen our revelationship, but these five are means of direct revelationship and should be welcomed, even desired (1 Cor. 12:31; 14:1).

Just as Jesus was "led by the Spirit" (Mt. 4:1; Lk. 2:27) and gave instructions "through the Spirit" (Acts 1:2), that same communication should continue in us as his representatives. We see an example of this during the trance and vision of Peter in Acts 10. In verse 19 of that chapter, the Holy Spirit spoke to Peter: "Simon, three men are looking for you." This revelation from the Holy Spirit gave specific, supernatural *knowledge* previously unknown to Peter. The Holy Spirit continued, "So get up and go downstairs. Do not hesitate to go with them, for I have sent them." This continued revelation of the Holy Spirit gave clear direction—or *wisdom*—on what to do. The first part was a word of knowledge; the second was a word

Ch. 4: The God Who Dwells among Us

of wisdom. These two gifts often work in tandem for communication from God.

Many years ago, when Christ revealed himself to me (Randy) in a dream, he challenged me about one of my greatest needs. His words were kind, but also full of authority. (I know what the temple guards meant when they said to the religious rulers, "No one ever spoke the way this man does" [John 7:46, NIV].) His words struck me to the core of my being. I awoke, trembling uncontrollably. But revelationship had deepened.

Not long ago, my (Randy's) son (and Cathy's brother) served in the U.S. infantry in Afghanistan. We often prayed for his safety, but one time our pastor's wife specifically prayed that he and his men would be invisible to the enemy. Shortly thereafter, my wife had a dream about angels encircling our son's squad and covering them with their wings. She awoke praying for his safety. Little did she know that these words of wisdom and prayers would be instrumental in protecting him and his men.

In fact, the strangest thing had happened. While on patrol, our son's squad was surrounded by the enemy. They could see the enemy all around, but the enemy did not see them. In a sense, the enemy was blind to their whereabouts. This continued for several days with our son's squad remaining invisible. When they finally radioed for help and gave their position, even the satellite could not locate them.

Do you remember the story of Elisha the prophet surrounded by the enemy at Dothan (2 Kings 6)? Elisha's servant looked out in the morning and saw an army of horses and chariots surrounding the city. His voice rang out in fear, "What shall we do?" But the prophet asked God to open the eyes of his servant to see the angelic forces around them, and he saw that the hills were full of angels. Then God struck the enemy with blindness so that they could not attack Elisha and his servant. Just as those angelic forces had protected Elisha, angelic forces had also protected my son and his men on patrol.

God sometimes reveals himself through the ways he protects us, as with Elisha, but at other times revelationship comes through the ways he sustains us in difficult times. As a Christian woman, I (Cathy) thought that if I followed the prescribed formula for marrying a "good Christian" man who was discipled and respected by the leaders of my church—as well as one who would put in the requisite hard work—I would have the family and marriage I longed for.

Unfortunately, after four years of marriage, I found myself abandoned, divorced, childless, wounded, and in debt. I felt desperate. I did everything "right" but still ended up with a failed marriage.

In response to my desperation, God called me aside to a cabin in the mountains where he spoke clearly to my heart. He gave me Isaiah 54, which promises children to the woman abandoned in her young marriage.

I held on to that through several years of an on-again-off-again relationship with the man who is now my second husband. He did not want children at the time, but even so, for my sake, he promised that one day we would have them.

I determined to wait patiently for God to fulfill Isaiah 54 for me rather than harangue my new husband into having them sooner rather than later. Not long after we married, God gave me a vision of two children—a boy and a girl, each holding one of my hands. Then the Holy Spirit placed his hands on my son's head, declaring his name to be Josiah and that he'd be the "last good thing to happen to Judah." I held on to that vision for many, many years.

Then, one day, my husband declared he was ready to have children. Eleven months and a miscarriage later, my son, Josiah, was born. Three years after that, my daughter, Cassia, was born. In my case, the promise from the Lord was the revelation I needed to sustain me through the long, childless years.

As God dwells among us through his Spirit, he also brings precious ministry gifts (Eph. 4:11, 1 Cor. 12:29), including apostles, prophets, evangelists, pastors, and teachers. Revelationship can occur when we recognize and make room for these gifts in others to operate within the Church. And we should not leave our discussion of the God who dwells among us without reviewing this aspect.

When the members of a local church recognize the passion and maturity within an individual for a given ministry—say pastoring, for example—and bless and promote the person in his or her service,[6] conditions develop for revelationship to occur in new and deeper ways. This happened in our local church when we released a husband and wife to launch a new church.

Here's how it happened. On the surface, this couple appeared content with their present, busy life, but they knew they were not being challenged to go deeper in their commitment and service to God. To some degree, they languished in their spiritual growth because of it.

God spoke to me clearly in a service one day that we had not implemented a process to raise up pastors

---

[6] Some protestant denominations select and promote leaders from within their local churches/parishes while the bishops of other faith traditions appoint them.

and plant churches. He let me know that we could do this even though we weren't a large church or part of a large denomination with a mature church planting program. He reminded me that part of our church heritage included planting churches organically—by building small groups and then sending them out as teams to start new churches. In fact, hundreds of churches had been started this way.

As I looked at this young man in that service, all these thoughts came back to me under the prompting of the Lord, and I knew that God was setting his hand on this couple and was asking me to call out the gifts within them. After meeting with them over the next few weeks, God spoke to them as well—as though "deep calls to deep"—and through many tears, the revelation of God's calling awakened in them.

Over the next four years, as training and preparation took place, their growth accelerated and their relationship with God deepened. All of this resulted from a demand placed on the anointing, a response to leadership responsibility, and a desperate need for God's help.

This resulted in revelationship. When God calls us and sets us apart to his work, he reveals himself in greater ways—each to meet the tasks ahead. Pastoral work uniquely requires revelationship. No pastor can succeed long without it.

This is the work of his grace—to meet our needs, whatever they may be—with whatever can be found in God's nature. He thus makes up for our lack. And he supplies that grace at the point of need. But each moment he reveals his grace, revelationship occurs. The greater the need, the greater the revelation of his presence. And at each moment that God supernaturally meets our needs, our faith increases for the next task at hand, especially those tasks that lie beyond our abilities.

Interestingly, even though sending a team immediately reduced church membership, the church experienced growth in the long term. Casting bread upon the waters always has a way of coming back home.

Finally, we should be aware that God's grace comes at the perfected moment of our need and not a single moment before. "From his abundance we have all received one gracious blessing after another" (John 1:16, NLT)—grace upon grace. Everything is provided for the journey but comes at the point of need so that we have continuous revelationship. This is how God dwells among us.

Journal Prompt: We are transformed when we are brought into God's presence by the power of the Holy Spirit. How do you make room for God's presence in your life?

Download our accompanying Devotional Study Guide for FREE at Revelationship.net. It contains mindful study questions, devotional cues, and journaling prompts to help you as chronicle God's revelations to you as he pursues you for a deeper relationship.

CHAPTER FIVE

THE GOD WHO WRESTLES WITH US

Then the man said, "Your name will no longer be Jacob, but Israel, because you have struggled with God and with humans and have overcome."

—Genesis 32:38 (NIV)

Have you ever wrestled with some issue with God—maybe over an offense with someone or a tough decision that must be made? I (Randy) have agonized with God over both. Sometimes it takes years to resolve the issues, but sometimes it just takes a few minutes of quiet prayer.

Often, after I'm in bed meditating on events of the day, I find myself struggling with God over some problem. He often keeps me awake until I hear from him. I toss and turn, knowing that something is unresolved, and I can't quite hear what the answer is. I may try to resolve it by my own thoughts, but that doesn't give me peace, so I toss and turn some more. Then it happens—the Lord pierces through and the revelation hits the mark.

One time he showed me that I needed to pray for someone who had hurt me deeply. By breaking through with this revelation, and praying for this person, the Lord set me free from my anger.

Another time, regarding a deeply troubling situation, I heard his words of wisdom to resolve the problem—thus releasing me from worry. When each revelation comes, peace also floods my soul and I immediately fall asleep.

Many times, I (Cathy) cannot sleep because of negative words spoken over me that day. I must wrestle them to the ground with the truth of what God declares about me. (Now, to avoid late-night wrestling, I've learned to simply confront the person speaking the curse in real-time, so I don't have to deal with it later.) Sometimes I wrestle with God as he asks me to surrender a fear or part of my identity to him. Other times, I toss and turn at an injustice I've heard or seen. Most of the time I simply must get to the place of absolute surrender—but sometimes he wrestles with me until I get up and do something about the injustice.

One time, someone said this about one of my sisters: "It's been months since she lost that pregnancy. She needs to move on!" I had to get up from bed and write a lengthy email calling the church to respond like Christ to those in mourning.

Another time, I had attended a shallow, ridiculous baby shower that was more of a show of wealth than a celebration of the woman and her soon-to-be-born child. It bothered me all night. In the early hours of the morning, I told my husband the situation and we decided that we needed to go to the woman and do what should have happened at the shower: anoint her and pray for her, binding any spirit of fear and releasing a fabulous delivery, as well as listen and declare what God had to say over the child's destiny.

Ch. 5: The God Who Wrestles with Us

When we turn to the Bible, the Psalms clearly show us that we are not alone in wrestling with God. These ancient lyrics often depict the author's struggles in such a transparent way that we sense they have wrestled long with God.

In one Psalm King David agonized over his transgressions to the point that he felt as though his bones were crushed (Ps. 51). Another time he felt forsaken by God (Ps. 22)—that God was far from the words of his groaning—causing him to cry out to God both day and night. Yet another time, David's guilt felt as though God pierced his soul with arrows (Ps. 38).

> At times like this—at the end of ourselves—God often meets with us. Jacob's manipulative spirit tainted all his thinking. Jacob needed a change in character and only an encounter with God—the God who wrestles with us—can break such life-dominating sin.

Do you remember the story of Jacob and how he wrestled (literally) with God? Jacob was at a crisis point in his life and was alone one night when the Lord wrestled with him.

Jacob, the schemer, who had tricked his brother out of the birthright and his father out of the blessing, now faced the impossible situation of returning home. Although he had accumulated many possessions by this time, he had sent them with his family in groups across the Jabbok Ford ahead of him in one last attempt to appease his brother. Esau was on his way to meet him with a large contingent of armed men!

Now Jacob was alone as night settled.

At times like this—at the end of ourselves—God often meets with us. Jacob's manipulative spirit tainted all his thinking. Jacob needed a change in character and only an encounter with God—the God who wrestles with us—can break such life-dominating sin.

That night, Jacob faced a man who stood in his way at the river ford. The two began to wrestle until they were down in the dust and dirt. The struggle occurred on the threshold of the Promised Land—the threshold of blessing. Jacob's manipulations had exiled him from the land of promise for years. Now God would not let him pass until he changed.

Jacob wrestled obstinately all night while the darkness concealed his adversary. Only when God touched Jacob's thigh and rendered him lame, did Jacob realize the awesome person of his adversary. And, in doing so, Jacob finally faced up to his own inability. He saw his own helplessness. He had finally come to the end of himself and recognized the real source of his blessings. As a result, he was limping in his flesh, but he was whole in spirit! God broke Jacob's physical strength but gave him inner peace.

God's revelation redeemed his past identity and transformed his future—all indicated in his new name, Israel.[7]

So it is with sin. It can exile us from revelationship. Eventually, God makes something so difficult in our lives that we have no choice but to deal with the sin. We come to the end of ourselves and, in anguish, we wrestle with God. In Jacob's case, God wanted to change him from being manipulative to one who is poor in spirit (Mt. 5:3)—to know that he needed God desperately. When we wrestle with God, we come to recognize that God has been there all along to direct, provide, and bless. He's the one truly in control!

Jacob refused to let go of his adversary until he received a blessing. This persistence is necessary when wrestling with God. We know that he has

---

[7] Genesis 32 and 33.

something for us, something to reveal to us, something desperately needed. Don't give up—wrestle until the revelation comes.

In fact, Hosea says that Jacob "wept and begged for his favor" (Hos. 12:4, NIV). Sometimes wrestling brings us to tears. And tears often come at the breaking point—the point of repentance.

That's when the revelation comes.

When God departed and Jacob (now Israel) crossed over the river at the Jabbok Ford, he crossed it with a limp. He could now face his brother, whom he had greatly offended, in humility and brokenness. But God gave him favor in his brother's eyes. They met and embraced each other and wept for joy.

Some of us have a Jabbok Ford to cross, but we haven't wrestled with God. We haven't come face to face with God and our own weakness. Perhaps some of us haven't really been in the blessings of God for years—self-exiled from his promises and his presence. We may need to wrestle with God until we receive the revelation we need to break through.

Journal Prompt: How has God changed you through times of wrestling with him or yourself?

Download our accompanying Devotional Study Guide for FREE at Revelationship.net. It contains mindful study questions, devotional cues, and journaling prompts to help you as chronicle God's revelations to you as he pursues you for a deeper relationship.

CHAPTER SIX

THE GOD WHO RESCUES US

In your righteousness deliver me and rescue me; incline your ear to me and save me.
—Psalm 71:22 (NIV)

Come with us for a few moments to an ancient Mediterranean coastal town of Zarephath, between Tyre and Sidon. Imagine a time when a three-year drought withered everything living and severe famine now ravished the land. A single mother—a widow—gathered sticks for a fire. She planned to cook the food she had for one last meal with her son. What she didn't know was that she was about to have an encounter with God—the God who rescues us.

God had already been working on the widow's behalf though that was unseen to her. He sent his prophet to work a miracle. While she gathered sticks, she met a stranger who asked her for water and then some bread. She had only enough for her

> We often do not see how God works things together on our behalf, until the revelation comes, and we are rescued. But he is working, nonetheless. For what often looks insurmountable to us, is merely an opportunity to God.

and her son, she explained. They would eat this as their last meal.

Then the promise of provision came: "The jar of flour will not be used up and the jug of oil will not run dry until the day the Lord gives rain on the land" (1 Ki 17:14, NIV). God met her at her point of need—and rescued her.

We often do not see how God works things together on our behalf, until the revelation comes, and we are rescued. But he is working, nonetheless. For what often looks insurmountable to us is merely an opportunity to God.

We may even count ourselves as too unimportant for God to notice. But to God, no one is inconsequential. In fact, as long as there is a Bible, the story of the widow of Zarephath will be remembered.

God revealed himself as the one who notices, the one who provides, and the one who rescues. He sent his prophet to perform a miracle and thereby relieve the downtrodden. His help can come in the most unexpected ways, by the most unexpected messengers. But it comes—again and again it comes. Until the famine ended, every time she poured oil from the jug or took some flour from the jar, a miracle took place.

Sometimes God's solution may not be what we expect or desire. (Wouldn't it be easier for God to simply end the famine?) But God's purposes are greater than ours. And we may not understand the "why" of things. Only he knows every ripple of consequence. Only he knows what revelation best meets the need—and how it may touch the lives of many others.

My (Randy's) wife was about two months pregnant with her first child and miscarried. The loss devastated her. To comfort her, the Lord gave her a remarkable vision of our son. As she was preparing dinner one evening, she saw her son as a young adult standing across from the kitchen. Of course, this helped heal her broken heart.

As a result of her vision, our family gave our son in heaven a name. We look forward to greeting him at the Lord's side. My wife has shared the story with many other women who have suffered miscarriages, and it has brought them similar comfort. Only a God who brings revelationship does such things.

I (Cathy), too, have experienced this God who brings very personal comfort to those who have lost children. My first and only pregnancy of my first marriage was a miscarriage. My first husband was ruthlessly relieved. I was heartbroken. It never healed.

Thirteen years later, married to a wonderful man but still childless, my family and I went on a vacation together. All my sisters and several of their husbands, my grandmother, my father's sister, my parents and I sat up late into the night intensely discussing revival and theology. When I went to bed, I felt the presence of God pursue me up the stairs.

As I laid down to sleep, God drew very close. He spoke to me, telling me it was time for me to name my son whom I had lost. (Until then, I was not sure what gender the child had been.) He gave me a glimpse of a red-headed, freckled, smiling urchin of a boy who, I instantly felt confident, loved music and composed it with my grandfather in heaven. That one glimpse healed 13 years of silent pain. Then, I asked God what my son's name was. He showed me "Aiden," which I later learned means "little fire." I look forward to knowing Aiden in heaven.

We should not be surprised that the Bible is full of examples of God personally rescuing his people. We find him using Joseph to save many lives from famine, including those of his own family. God's foreknowledge of the coming disaster caused him to work on behalf of everyone through the ups and downs of Joseph's life. All along there was revelationship through the dreams of Joseph and his ability to interpret the dreams of others. Throughout the story lies an undercurrent of Joseph's trust in God.

The Bible often celebrates the Exodus of the nation of Israel out of slavery in Egypt. Before this took place, the hand of God moved on Israel's behalf by an outpouring of plagues on Egypt until Pharaoh exclaimed, "Enough!" Moses' revelationship of a God in a miraculous burning bush—a God who spoke to him and performed miracles through him—broke through to rescue a nation.

The Psalms record how David often prayed for God to rescue him and the people of Israel from their enemies. And while Jesus called us to respond differently toward our enemies than the Psalmists, we can certainly agree with David that "he has prepared a table before me in the presence of my enemies" (Psalm 23:5, NIV).

The greatest rescue known to humankind, of course, came through Jesus' death on a cross for our sins. His sinless sacrifice redeemed us—purchased salvation for us. Even here there is abundant revelationship, for the apostle John says, "[Even though] no one has ever seen God, the unique God, the One in deepest, closest connection with the Father, has revealed him" (John 1:18, personal translation). Throughout his life, all that Jesus does and says derives from and reveals the Father. In fact, Jesus exemplified such complete union with the Father that he could claim, "Anyone who has seen me has seen the Father" (Jn. 14:9, NIV).

Do you remember the movie *Ben Hur*—the one starring Charleton Heston? Remember the remarkable scene where Ben Hur saw the leper colony for the first time and was gripped by the monstrous inhumanity to these outcasts of society? In a very moving scene, he ignores the dangers to himself and heads hell-bent deep into the caves searching for his leprous sister, Tirzah. When he finds her, he gathers her in his arms—despite her protests—to bring her home. One would be hard-pressed to find a better illustration of Christ, who sought us in the dark recesses of sin and rescued us from certain death.

Even Christ, alone among all those of the crowd, reached out his hand to touch the leper. No glove—just bare skin against raw, open sores. How rare that must have been for the leper—the soft touch—the hand of compassion—the hand of healing! Here was the Good Shepherd leaving the ninety-nine to find the lost one.

Jesus loved us "to the end" (Jn. 13:1), laying down his life for us. He thereby brings us into that union of the Father and Son as close as possible (Jn. 17:21-22).

This is revelationship: God is there. He is aware. And he pursues us until he rescues us.

Journal Prompt: The first call we hear is when God calls us from darkness into his glorious light, rescuing us from blindness and exile. Take a moment to remember life before he first rescued you and thank him for the life he freely gives.

Download our accompanying Devotional Study Guide for FREE at Revelationship.net. It contains mindful study questions, devotional cues, and journaling prompts to help you as chronicle God's revelations to you as he pursues you for a deeper relationship.

CHAPTER SEVEN

THE GOD WHO DISTURBS US

"I form light and create darkness, I make well-being and create calamity, I am the Lord, who does all these things."

—Isaiah 45:7 (NIV)

Supposing Jesus walked into a Sunday service in a typical American church, and everyone recognized him. Would he be told to sit in the back and not say anything? Would we allow him to interrupt the service—or would we insist on our schedule? If Jesus presented himself, would we not give him all the time he needed? Would we not, in fact, sit at his feet and hear what is on his heart?

Why do we not give the Holy Spirit the same opportunity? Yet every Sunday in churches all over America, we corral the Spirit. We banish him to afterglow meetings or rush through the service without the gifts of the Spirit. Why? Probably because the Spirit ministers through people. And that gets messy. Probably because the Spirit comes like fire. And that disturbs us.

Ch. 7: The God Who Disturbs Us

Yet, it was a glorious disturbance at Pentecost when the Spirit fell like tongues of fire (Acts 2:1-4). It was a great disturbance when the disciples prayed, and the place was shaken as they were filled

> The priority should be the pursuit of God's presence and the deepening of relationship with him. A church that does not answer God's question, "Where are you?" is a church with the wrong priorities.

with the Spirit (Acts 4:31). When Paul describes a service in the New Testament, he says that the unbeliever should be so disturbed in his heart because of the prophetic word that falling down and worshiping he will exclaim, "God is really among you!" (1 Corinthians 14:25, NIV).

Instead, we pamper visitors and banish the Spirit.

Where is the prophetic word? Where is the conviction? The power? The challenge? The disturbance?

If his Presence doesn't bring us to our knees in the twenty minutes we allow for worship, why do we stop? If his Presence is driven from the service, why do we even gather? I (Cathy) have a saying: If God doesn't show up for your service, why should I? What could possibly be more important than his Presence? What on earth have we settled for?

Sure, we should desire order in the service. But there is order in a graveyard, too—just not much life.

When a local gathering of believers pursues God's presence, his presence distinguishes that local church from any other social group, just as his presence set the Israelites apart from all other nations. Unfortunately, for many churches in the West, the focus centers on a brief worship service and a sermon. Thus, revelationship comes in only these two avenues during the service. Unfortunately, most church attendees learn that these are the only two ways to experience God's presence.

The priority should be the pursuit of God's presence and the deepening of relationship with him. A church that does not answer God's question, "Where are you?" is a church with the wrong priorities.

A. W. Tozer once said, "Current evangelicalism has...laid the altar and divided the sacrifice into parts, but now seems satisfied to count the stones and rearrange the pieces with never a care that there is not a sign of fire upon the top of lofty Carmel." But God is the God who answers by fire (1 Kings 18:4).

Much of the Church today has found a way to tame God through a peculiar doctrine called dispensationalism. In a nutshell, this doctrine states that God has ceased with the gifts of the Spirit today—during this "dispensation." It is, in fact, nothing more than an interpretive grid placed over Scripture (not derived from it) to filter out the miraculous—to filter out most pathways to revelationship. It is nothing more than a way to tame God—a way to make him in our own preferred image.

Like the circus lion driven back to its stool by a whip and a chair, the Church has tried to tame the wildness out of God. Yet he won't be tamed. Miracles still happen. Healings still take place. The Lord still speaks to us in numerous ways. We crack our whip, but he's roaring elsewhere.

I am reminded of the way C. S. Lewis put this in his fantasy book, *The Lion, the Witch, and the Wardrobe*. New to the land of Narnia, a place where animals can talk, the Pevensie children are told about Aslan, the king of Narnia, who was, in fact, a large lion.

"Ooh!" said Susan, "I'd thought he was a man. Is he—quite safe? I shall feel rather nervous about meeting a lion."

"That you will dearie, and make no mistake," said Mrs Beaver; "if there's anyone who can appear before

Aslan without their knees knocking, they're either braver than most or else just silly."

"Then he isn't safe?" said Lucy.

"Safe!" said Mr. Beaver; "don't you hear what Mrs. Beaver tells you? Who said anything about safe? 'Course he isn't safe. But he's good. He's the King I tell you."

Several years ago, a close friend of our family, who was a nurse, attended a medical mission to South America with some pediatric doctors. At the mission event, people from around the area brought their children for medical attention. The doctors had arranged lines for those who would be examined and those who would receive prayer.

Our friend recounted to us how one young girl came forward to be examined. Her arm had been broken in the past, but because the bone had been set incorrectly, it left a bulging deformity along her arm. The doctors assessed it but told her to go to the prayer line because, other than surgery beyond their capability, there was nothing they could do medically to repair the bone, now permanently set.

As she went to receive prayer, a commotion began around those who were being prayed for. Several brought the young girl excitedly back to the doctors and nurses. The doctor examined her arm again and found it to be perfectly straight! Our friend said, "How is this possible?" The doctor replied, "That is the power of prayer."

Aslan had roared. God's presence had disturbed everything—gloriously disturbed everything. And he had revealed himself to all those who were there.

Journal Prompt: How can we invite more of the Holy Spirit to minister in our churches?

Download our accompanying Devotional Study Guide for FREE at Revelationship.net. It contains mindful study questions, devotional cues, and journaling prompts to help you as chronicle God's revelations to you as he pursues you for a deeper relationship.

FREE DOWNLOAD!

DEVOTIONAL GUIDE & WORKBOOK

REVELATIONSHIP.NET

CHAPTER EIGHT

REVELATIONSHIP THROUGH PRAYER AND THE GOD WHO HEALS US

And if we know that he hears us—whatever we ask—we know that we have what we asked of him.
—John 5:15 (NIV)

Not all prayers are life-and-death prayers, obviously, but far too many Christians pray only rarely, as a last resort, or lack the know-how to pray effectively. For many Christians, prayer is a to-do list or the last thing on a to-do list. Still others pray like a machine gun, hoping that a stray bullet of their prayers will hit the target and God will move on their behalf. Few pray with faith.

Christian's lack of faith stems, more than anything, from a lack of a revelationship with the God who answers prayers. They have not known (or taken the time to know) the revelation of the God who desires us to pray, desires to move on our behalf, and the God who intercedes for us while we pray.

In our experience, prayer is not begging God for a miracle, but about listening to what he wants to do and how he wants to move, then simply moving forward in faith with what he has revealed. Prayer requires a prophetic heart. It requires that we wait on God to receive the heart of God for the situation, then once he has revealed his heart, to declare it here on earth in faith. It requires revelationship.

During my (Cathy's) pregnancies, I prayed specifically over every aspect of my unborn child—organs, systems, destiny, habits—everything. What started as a way to focus my mind to fight against fear developed into a deep conviction that whatever God brought to my mind to pray for, he would grant. I even prayed that my son would have a good memory

> *Christian's lack of faith stems, more than anything, from a lack of a revelationship with the God who answers prayers. They have not known (or taken the time to know) the revelation of the God who desires us to pray, desires to move on our behalf, and the God who intercedes for us while we pray.*

Ch. 8: Revelationship through Prayer

and quick recall...I was very specific, and I had about 270 days to pray for something different each day!

When I held my healthy baby boy in my arms, I was overwhelmed with gratitude. In the days after, God used my gratefulness for my son's health to birth in me a ministry and burden for babies who are not born healthy and whole.

As a start in this ministry, I began to follow a child on Facebook who needed prayer. I became aware of this child through a friend. This led to others on Facebook, and soon I was joining groups that mothers of needy children had created to ask for prayer. Then, the following January, I joined others in praying for a young woman from my hometown whose daughter had been born with dire heart conditions, praying through their many trials with them and for them. That led to connecting with and praying for other children with congenital heart defects as the mothers reached out on Facebook for prayer.

That expanded to children with failing kidneys, livers, skin diseases, and even cancer.

The Lord taught me how to pray for these children: specifically and effectively. If a mother asked for prayer for her child's A1C to rise to a certain level, I would ask God for authority to pray for that specifically. If I heard him grant it, I prayed for it. Up the A1C rose. If a mother didn't know what to ask for specifically, I learned to ask God what he wanted me to pray for, or what to declare over the child, or what to command the child's body to do. If I heard something, I prayed for it, declared it, or commanded it.

Through these years, I have seen miracle after specific miracle. Once, a mother posted, "Pray! The doctors have said that if my daughter doesn't get a kidney match today, she will not last the night. We have been praying for a miracle for two years and time has run out!" I hit the ground on my knees to ask the Lord for permission to pray for a kidney

Ch. 8: Revelationship through Prayer   97

match. When he granted permission, I prayed for the match, following his lead to pray for "red tape" to be removed, for the organ itself to be in good condition when it arrived, for the child's system to accept and not reject it, and, of course, for comfort for the family of the one whose kidney was now to come to this child.

Then, when I felt the Holy Spirit release me from the burden to pray (about 15 minutes later), I rose, messaged the mom that I had just prayed and felt confident of an answer. She immediately messaged me back: "They just came in the room to tell us the kidney is on its way!!!"

This kind of thing has happened too many times to recount, even though I journaled my prayers for the children so I could look back and celebrate the miracles. A few times, however, God didn't give me permission to pray for healing of organs, and the child died. Those were the hardest to go through and

I cried at the loss of these children and the pain of their parents in their posts on Facebook. Sometimes I stubbornly prayed for healing just because my heart wanted it so badly, even when I knew I didn't have the authority to do so. God gently led me through those times, teaching me to only pray what he tells me to pray—nothing more, nothing less. (Though I sometimes still struggle to hear him if I'm really close to the person and want healing more than I want to hear God. That makes it far more difficult for me to hear God.)

Now, when I pray for a child in a life-and-death situation, I ask the Lord, "Will you declare this child will live and not die?" He almost always declares that they will live. Then I proceed in full confidence in his fulfilling his own declaration. After the declaration of life, everything else is a breeze.

Once, a professor friend of mine messaged me to tell me his son's wife had just birthed a child moments before, and it was born without blood (a fetal-maternal hemorrhage). The doctors gave the child zero chance of survival because of this and the child's non-response to testing. I immediately asked God if he would declare the child would live and not die. He did so and even showed me a quick vision of the son as an adult, playing guitar on a stage proclaiming God's goodness.

Armed with that vision, the Lord led me through each organ and system in the child's body, commanding it to "live and not die." He led me to pray specifically for the child to nurse and demonstrate a will to survive. I then prayed for his blood cells, marrow cells, brain cells, and a few things I can't even recall knowing about until God said to pray for them! A full hour later, I felt the release of the Holy Spirit. When my friend reached out again, he said that the baby had been nursed and that the doctors had completely reversed their prognosis.

Another time, all the doctors in the nation had given up on a young girl's heart. It was just too messed up for anyone to attempt anything else. They sent her home to die, but the mother refused. I had been following her for a while, praying for her daughter through several procedures and watching her escape death several times.

Finally, the Lord led me to pray for a specialist to receive wisdom from heaven and to take her case. One did! But he was in California and commercial airlines will not fly these sick little children. I joined others in praying for a flight, and a wealthy citizen provided their own private jet.

They asked us to pray for her to survive the flight and be healthy enough to have immediate surgery. I prayed that she would rally and that the doctors would be inspired by her inner strength enough to proceed. And that's what God did! She had the experimental surgery and is still alive today.

Sometimes the prayer requests resulted in miraculous healing of specific organs and other times for healing through the doctor's specific procedures. Other times it was to release wisdom from heaven for the doctors or to release grace for the parents who were fighting for their child's life. Other times it was for God to strategically move people and organizations into place to bring about a miracle.

Jesus desires us to pray, desires to move on our behalf, and is himself praying with us while we pray (Romans 8:34).

Journal Prompt: Have you ever thought about what it might mean to pray "unceasingly" while you go about your daily life?

Download our accompanying Devotional Study Guide for FREE at Revelationship.net. It contains mindful study questions, devotional cues, and journaling prompts to help you as chronicle God's revelations to you as he pursues you for a deeper relationship.

CHAPTER NINE

THE GOD WHO WHISPERS TO THE HURTING

The Lord is close to the brokenhearted and saves those who are crushed in spirit.

—Psalm 34:18 (NIV)

On June 29, 2006—on the day of my (Randy's) wedding anniversary—I closed the lid on the last packing box from my office in the church I had served for 26 years. Several days previous, the senior pastor had told me to clean out my desk by the end of the week.

This was the church I had sacrificed so much for—with finances, with time, with teaching. Over the years, God transformed me in many ways from a teacher into a pastor—caring for the sheep in so many tender ways. Do you know what it is like to sit across from parents and hear their moans at the loss of a son through suicide? (That's when the difficult questions come.) Or to oversee funeral arrangements—the service—the coffin—stories of loved ones now gone? Their eyes betray the question "Why?" but all you can do is pray that God's presence will be ever close. When I faced these pastoral situations, I would shut my office door, and there, on my knees, listen for God's heart. God would wrench my heart apart with compassion to prepare me to pastor families in those difficult times.

However, during my years of sacrifice, there was a growing conflict with the senior pastor. The disagreements came to a head. So, I handed in my resignation—alone—thinking that I would probably never be back.

Have you ever been in such a dark place: "the cave"? A place of loneliness, despair, and dejection. That day I entered the cave. That day relationships were broken. In fact, I can count on one hand the number of members from the church who reached out to me during that time. The friends were painfully missed.

That day the church lost its pastor.

Shortly after this, I received a letter from the minister's fellowship I belonged to letting me know that I was no longer a member. They sent a form letter—

no courtesy of an exit interview—and let me know that I shouldn't take it personally. Insult to injury.

That day I lost a job and faced the uncertainty of unemployment, ending up with a $35,000-a-year pay cut. Then the church cut in half the severance package I was promised.

Living in a cave is not fun.

Elijah, David, and Daniel were all in "caves" at one point in their lives. During the reign of King Ahab, all the remaining Lord's prophets were hidden in a cave. I wonder if Job felt like he was in a "cave." Jonah was swallowed by a "cave" that swam. Jesus' friend Lazarus was laid to rest in a cave. He was there three days before Jesus called him out. And even Jesus was buried in a cave—a tomb cut out of rock.

Do you remember Elijah and his experience with a cave? After the "mountaintop" experience of triumphing over the prophets of Baal (1 Kings 19:1-18) came the "cave" experience when Jezebel threatened his life. Elijah was broken. It must have seemed to him like no matter what he did, in the end, it wouldn't matter. You can serve God spectacularly, and still be rejected. Elijah was ready to turn in his prophet's badge and write his resignation: "I have had enough, Lord…"

It is often in times of disappointment, rejection—even depression—that we see our needs the most. Have you lost your job? A ministry? A church? A loved one? Have you ever said you've had enough? Life's trials are too much for us without God's help—without his grace. The journey was too much for Elijah, it can be too much for us. You cannot make it through the dark places alone.

> Then God's voice wasn't in the wind, the earthquake, or the fire—not this time. Instead, he spoke in a still, small voice. God's presence doesn't always come in spectacular ways. He often whispers to us, especially when we are hurting.

When cavern walls surround you, remember that God has not abandoned you. God was with Elijah, and he will be with you, too. He met Elijah's needs for the journey through an angel, who provided him with food and drink. When Elijah arrived at the cave on Mount Horeb, he was still not alone. God spoke to him in a still, small voice, thus continuing revelationship.

God's first words directly to Elijah, "Why are you here?" caused him to take stock of his situation. Elijah's response is one of desperation and a little self-pity. But he poured out his complaint to God; and we should, too.

Then God's voice wasn't in the wind, the earthquake, or the fire—not this time. Instead, he spoke in a still, small voice. God's presence doesn't always come in spectacular ways. He often whispers to us, especially when we are hurting.

God then told Elijah to go and minister to Elisha and anoint others. He gave Elijah hope and directed him out of the cave—out of depression—by ministering to others. The best way out of a cave is to obey God and minister to others. If you sit and wallow in your self-pity and anger, you will never come out of the cave. Hear what God says: get up and begin to minister again.

I had to do that. I couldn't allow myself to sit in the cave—in the darkness. I had to hear from God. And slowly, sometimes painfully, I found myself in the daylight again. God is never done with you. God doesn't just commission, he also re-commissions.

Elijah's "cave" experience refined his character and deepened his relationship with God more than any mountaintop experience had ever done. God will do the same for you.

David, too, was in a cave, far away from the Lord's temple, wrongly treated by King Saul. Joseph started his true destiny in a cistern. Falsely accused, Daniel was thrown into the lion's den. But God was with them all.

Never forget that Christ went to the cave already for you. And he rose from the grave—out of the cave! Whether we are unjustly treated, rejected, alone, depressed, downcast, lonely, dejected…no matter what our cave, Christ has gone into the cave to bring us out!

Journal Prompt: Have you ever had a "cave" experience? What happened? How did God bring you out?

Download our accompanying Devotional Study Guide for FREE at Revelationship.net. It contains mindful study questions, devotional cues, and journaling prompts to help you as chronicle God's revelations to you as he pursues you for a deeper relationship.

Ch. 9: The God Who Whispers to the Hurting

TEN

REVELATIONSHIP IN NATURE

For since the creation of the world his invisible attributes, his eternal power and divine nature, have been clearly seen, being understood through what has been made, so that they are without excuse.
—Romans 1:20 (NIV)

My (Randy's) favorite poem is *The Windhover* by Gerard Manley Hopkins. In it Hopkins celebrates the majesty of God in nature by the falcon's "riding"—"how he rung upon the rein of a wimpling wing"—and by the colors revealed in the shine of "sillion" turned up by a plow. Hopkins deeply understood revelationship with God through nature.

"Day unto day" nature speaks to us of the glory of God, the Psalmist declared (Psalm 19:1-4). The beauty of God's character is everywhere revealed in nature. It transcends every language. It has so much to say to us if we only have ears to hear or eyes to see as Hopkins did.

> In nature, we find the intricacies of the human eye, the aerodynamics of maple seeds, and the amazing colors of seashells. We find the language of a designer in all these and his fingerprints in the DNA of all creatures. In nature we find revelationship with God.

When we tread into the arena of nature's revelation, we cannot do so as scientists, mechanically gathering data. Nor are we on a Walden Pond nature excursion. Instead, we explore nature as those who have a personal relationship with Jesus and know without a doubt that he is the Creator. In our quest to know him, we want to hear his voice resound from the grandeur of every mountain, the lashing of every wave, and the stillness of a starry night.

In nature, we find the intricacies of the human eye, the aerodynamics of maple seeds, and the amazing colors of seashells. We find the language of a designer in all these and his fingerprints in the DNA of all creatures. In nature, we find revelationship with God.

Gary Thomas in *Sacred Pathways* shares that the Bible is meant to be read outdoors, explaining that many of its illustrations and allusions gain full meaning and force when experienced outdoors. He also points out that many of the Old Testament theophanies happened in the wilderness: with Hagar, Abraham, Jacob, and Moses.

We are reminded of the life of Jonathan Edwards, who regularly took rides in nature. One day he even experienced a vision of the Lord:

> Once, as I rode out into the woods for my health, in 1737, having alighted from my horse in a retired place, as my manner commonly has been, to walk in divine contemplation and prayer, I had a view that was for me extraordinary...I saw the glory of the Son of God, as Mediator between God and man, and his wonderful, great, full, pure and sweet grace and love, and meek and gentle condescension.
>
> This grace that appeared so calm and sweet, appeared also great above the heavens.

The person of Christ appeared ineffably excellent, with an excellency great enough to swallow up all thought and conception—which continued, as near as I can judge, about an hour.

This kept me the greater part of the time in a flood of tears, and weeping aloud. I felt an ardency of soul to be, what I know not otherwise how to express, emptied and annihilated.

I wanted to lie in the dust, and to be full of Christ alone; to love him with a holy and pure love; to trust in him, to live upon him, to serve and follow him, and to be perfectly sanctified and made pure with a divine and heavenly purity.[8]

---

[8] *The Works of Jonathan Edwards*, Vol 1, p. xlvii

Ch. 10: Revelationship in Nature

I (Cathy) find that the outdoors provides the best place for object lessons (just as Jesus did). Just as my father did for me, I point out to my children the details and artistry in nature my eyes are trained to see, using them to convey the spiritual lessons of nature: allowing time to wonder about the Creator, visualizing scriptural truths so they embed in our hearts, seeing God more clearly, and learning to rest.

I often feel God revealed himself to me through the plants, trees, mountains, and especially the beach. As a city girl, I was lucky to have what seemed like miles of wood beyond the fence of our backyard. My brother and I would tromp through it for hours, discovering everything from tadpoles to patches of poison ivy, before hearing my mother call us in for dinner. Later, my time in nature became limited as I grew up and spent more time being busy inside.

When I was thirteen, I spent my first day at the beach and was hooked. I become a different person at the beach (according to my husband, anyway). The beach creates margin in me, and the constant wind blows away the broken loops (incomplete tasks) and stressors in my mind. God always speaks to me when I've created margin—usually somewhere out in nature.

Once, when I had been divorced from my first husband and close to burnout (I busied myself working for the church to avoid facing pain), God broke into my devotions, demanding rather loudly that I "Come away" with him. His voice was like a hammer in my mind, persistent as a dripping faucet, until I made the decision to drive to my uncle's lake house in the North Georgia mountains—in the middle of a snowstorm. Once there, God "downloaded" volumes to me, speaking clearly and at length. I journaled for hours. I prayed and cried for still more. In the end, God sealed Isaiah 54 to my heart, promising that one day I would indeed have children and a family. I hung on to this promise for over ten years. Just as he did for others, God broke in when I made the space for him. And a large part of that had to do with meeting him in nature hushed by a snowstorm.

Another time, I experienced God's breaking in while surrounded by family at St. George Island. There were no lights for miles around us (lights at night are illegal because of turtle activity) and no lights were on the ocean in front of us. So, the sky was filled with the Milky Way.

We were overcome. We reclined out on the deck on the island, just looking up at the majesty of God for hours.

Prior to this, since I grew up in Atlanta near the airport, I had *no idea* what a sky full of stars looked like. Frankly, I was unimpressed by the handful of stars I saw typically at night. I had absolutely no idea what others meant when they wrote about a starry night—until then. Now Psalm 19:1 made sense: "The heavens declare the glory of God; the skies proclaim the work of his hands" (NIV).

I am reminded of the following lyrics from the popular hymn, *How Great Thou Art*:

> When through the woods and forest glades I wander
> And hear the birds sing sweetly in the trees;
> When I look down from lofty mountain grandeur
> And hear the brook and feel the gentle breeze;
> Then sings my soul, my Savior God, to thee,
> How great thou art, how great thou art![9]

Unfortunately, I'm not alone in my latent ability to appreciate and meet God in creation. We like chaos and busyness because it distracts us from ourselves. And the American Church, in its current state, is not much help here—there's not much place for

---

[9] Lyrics to *How Great Thou Art* by Stuart K. Hine.

the disciplines of solitude and silence, and we're not taught these.

Instead, we find silence deafening and solitude terrifying. When we do get out in creation, and the sounds of nature have quelled our stressors to silence, we're left with our own voices. It's here that we grapple with what we've been keeping at bay—pushed to the periphery—and God breaks in.

Sure, God, in his mercy, breaks in at any time, but being out in nature makes it easier for him to do so. (Maybe this is why God was able to break in to reveal himself to Paul, out on the road to Damascus, not in the busy metropolis of Jerusalem.)

As a busy mom and businesswoman, I must build outdoor time into my schedule because I am not normally a naturalist. I'm a doer and homebody. And I hate heat, humidity, bugs, gnats, and cold weather, but I'm convinced of the need to program time to wonder at creation.

"Martin Luther tells us that it is only with the "eye of faith" that we can see miracles all through nature, miracles that he believed were even greater than the miracles of the sacraments. If we truly understood the growth of a grain of wheat, he says we would die of wonder."[10]

If we don't appreciate creation, we can't fully appreciate the Creator. We must learn to seek the Creator behind the creation, which Martin Luther called the "mask of God," partially concealing yet revealing the Creator for the one who seeks him.

> "Earth's crammed with heaven, and every common bush afire with God; but only he who sees, takes off his shoes, the rest sit round it and pluck blackberries." —Elizabeth Barret Browning

---

[10] Gary Thomas, *Sacred Pathways* (Grand Rapids: Zondervan, 2010), 52.

Now I train my children to appreciate the beautiful lacework that our Creator places on the backs of every leaf, yet few stop to appreciate it because leaves are so plentiful. I help them see the God who creates beauty because he likes it, regardless of whether we appreciate it. I show them to the grains of crushed seashells that make up the beach and how the Bible says God thinks more thoughts of us than there are grains of sand. And point them to the Artist who paints details on the seashells that are not "necessary" or "utilitarian."

So, I adjust my busy-mom ways to make sure I properly appreciate the flecks of "gold" in the pockets full of rocks my son brings home, the million-dollar-dinosaur-tooth, or the bent twist of the "awesome" stick my son hid in his shorts all day long to bring home to me. (I cannot fathom how uncomfortable that must have been.) To appreciate every acorn my son brings home and every dandelion my daughter picks for me. I adjust my aversion to the "dirtiness" of the feathers they find outside and grit my teeth to pick up the dead Luna moth because I know my son will adore it.

I close my laptop and go walking in the garden.

In nature, will he not be to us "...a billion times told lovelier, more dangerous, O my chevalier!"?

Journal Prompt: What can you do more to appreciate God through his creation? How can you pass this on to your children and grandchildren?

Download our accompanying Devotional Study Guide for FREE at Revelationship.net. It contains mindful study questions, devotional cues, and journaling prompts to help you as chronicle God's revelations to you as he pursues you for a deeper relationship.

ELEVEN

REVELATIONSHIP THROUGH COVENANT

Know therefore that the Lord your God is God; he is the faithful God, keeping his covenant of love to a thousand generations of those who love him and keep his commandments.

—Deuteronomy 7:9 (NIV)

Late one night long, long ago, after a worshipper had offered his animal sacrifice and fallen asleep, he was awakened by a strange sight. Over his sacrifice appeared a "smoking firepot and a blazing torch" which then passed between the pieces of the sacrifice. At that moment, God "cut" covenant with Abram and spoke to him of his plan to give his descendants the Promised Land. By using this very ancient, symbolic act of passing through the pieces of the sacrifice, God was, in fact, guaranteeing this promise with his very being (Jeremiah 34:18-20)!

This firepot and torch represented God's presence, his acceptance of the sacrifice, and demonstrated that fellowship with him occurs through covenant. Divine covenants (that is, covenants between God and humankind) are how God establishes and maintains revelationship with us. Divine covenants enable us to step into the reciprocal, intimate relationship with God our hearts long for. Without covenants, we are left with nothing to bridge the sin-gap between us and God. Without covenants, the parameters of relationships are undefined. But through the means of divine covenants, God's grace extends to us through the shedding of blood, thus atoning for our sin and enabling fellowship to ensue.

So much are divine covenants about revelationship with God that the Bible depicts them in the intensely personal terms of a husband-and-wife relationship (Jeremiah 31:32; Ezekiel 16; Hosea). Loyalty, commitment, and love are frequently used in the Bible to describe covenant relationship with God, just as in a marriage covenant. Breaking the covenant terms meant that the person had "broken faith" with God (as with a marriage partner). But, even more importantly, just as marriage partners learn deeply about each other through the covenant relationship, so God desires to reveal himself to the divine covenant participants. He did this with Abram (later "Abraham") as well as with Moses and David, and the nation of Israel.

Divine covenants were often celebrated with a meal at their inauguration, just like marriage covenant celebrations, thus promoting fellowship. Isn't it remarkable that the elders of Israel sat down with the Lord (Ex. 24:9-11) to celebrate their covenant with a meal? In fact, the sacrificial system instituted by Moses was meant to provide fellowship between the worshipper, who partook of the sacrifice, and God, whose portion was (symbolically) consumed on the altar (Lev. 3:11; 7:15-18).

Of all the divine covenants revealed in the Bible, the most important is the final New Covenant. This covenant enables the closest possible relationship to

God by filling partakers with the Holy Spirit himself—the personal, divine presence of God.

Through the Spirit, the New Covenant provides what was missing under the old covenants—the power to live a godly life. It opens the heavenlies to our intercession (Hebrews 4:16), where we can draw near to the Lord (Hebrews 10:22), thus enabling us to have the thrilling opportunity to know him in his current ministry to the Church.

Further, the New Covenant ordinance of communion not only commemorates the death, burial, and resurrection of Jesus, but also reminds us of our current fellowship with him (and one another as his Body), and the future fellowship believers share as we partake of the Lord's table.[11] Without debating the

---

[11] See Isaiah 25:6; Matthew 8:11; 26:29, Luke 14:15-24; Revelation 19:7-9.

various views on how Christ is present during communion, Christians can agree that relationship is at the heart of the matter.

This New Covenant with Christ also requires loyalty and commitment (Matthew 10:37) from all participants. Without these qualities, there can be no revelationship. And loyalty and commitment build trust—an essential ingredient for any lasting relationship. In fact, the deeper the covenant loyalty and commitment, the deeper the trust grows. This provides the soil in which revelationship can take root and flourish.

> This is what we've been saying all along: At the heart of relationship-building is revelation. We know intrinsically that developing relationships with others means revealing yourself to them (in godly ways, of course). It is so natural that we hardly give it a thought.

The covenant of marriage illustrates this. God designed each step of the relationship to deepen as the engaged couple commit further to each other. As they do this, the couple trusts one another with more revelation about each other. Ultimately, the relationship leads to the final step of the marriage covenant where two pledge mutual and unbroken commitment during the marriage ceremony. After taking this final step, the husband and wife reveal the most open, most vulnerable, and most intimate revelation of each other in the marriage bed.

This is what we've been saying all along: At the heart of relationship-building is revelation. We know intrinsically that developing relationships with others means revealing yourself to them (in godly ways, of course). It is so natural that we hardly give it a thought.

In contrast to the loyalty necessary to maintain a marriage covenant, today's idea of "hooking up" or "sleeping together" before marriage violates the true nature of revelationship, the kind God intended. Instead, intercourse in such shallow relationships is often expected—even demanded—without any mutual loyalty or commitment. No wonder marriages are so fragile today. There is nothing to protect what each spouse revealed in the relationship. There is no commitment beyond meeting selfish desires.

The marriage covenant is not just about finding happiness or about obtaining a cure for loneliness. It illustrates how to have revelationship with God and how God wants us to handle revelationship with one another in marriage. Through marriage, the husband and wife place into the hands of the other spouse the sacred trust of intimacy.

In a similar violation, pornography usurps godly revelationship in favor of selfish lusts. The pornographic pictures offer a false sense of intimacy without any commitment whatsoever. This form of idolatry results in hindering true revelationship with God. However, when the pictures from the past come to mind, the temptation can be overcome by praying for the persons as God sees them and letting relationship with the Lord cleanse the heart and mind.

Likewise, adultery not only breaks the marriage covenant—thus undermining commitment and trust with the marriage partner—but also results in intercourse with the adulterer without lasting commitment and trust. Those who think they can have a godly, intimate relationship with more than one person, and still have trust and deep commitment, are merely deceiving themselves.

Just as God committed his whole being to the covenant relationship with Abram, he did so on the cross through Jesus Christ for New Covenant believers. God then entrusts us with revelationship through this New Covenant. In the same way, the husband and wife entrust one another with revelationship through the marriage covenant.

Journal Prompt: Does knowing that God swore to keep the covenant by his own power—we clearly weren't going to be able to do so—free you to experience his presence without attempting to earn it?

Download our accompanying Devotional Study Guide for FREE at Revelationship.net. It contains mindful study questions, devotional cues, and journaling prompts to help you as chronicle God's revelations to you as he pursues you for a deeper relationship.

CHAPTER TWELVE

REVELATIONSHIP THROUGH SUFFERING AND THE GOD WHO WANTS OUR WHOLE LIFE

Then Jesus told his disciples, "If anyone would come after me, let him deny himself and take up his cross and follow me."

—Matthew 16:24 (NIV)

"For eighty-six years I have been his servant, and he has done me no wrong. How can I blaspheme my King who saved me?"[12] These were the words of Polycarp, the Bishop of Smyrna, and Early Church father. He confessed this just before he was martyred—burned at the stake—when asked to deny that he was a Christian. He considered himself an "acceptable sacrifice" and praised the Lord to be found worthy of martyrdom.

We can only imagine the kind of pressure the threat of martyrdom brings—to either deny Jesus or be killed. Throughout the history of the Church, there have been martyrs. One only has to glance through the classic *Foxe's Book of Martyrs* to be

---

[12] Michael W. Holmes, editor and translator, *The Apostolic Fathers: Greek Text and English Translations*, third edition *Martyrdom of Polycarp* 9:3 (Grand Rapids, Baker, 2007), 317.

amazed at those who have remained true to Christ amid ultimate adversity. And there are many, many, even today, that pay this price.

Polycarp illustrates what it means to live a life entirely yielded to God. Long before he faced his final trial, he was already a "living sacrifice" (Romans 12:1). In truth, before any believer can face the flames of the martyr's pyre, they must have long resolved that their life belongs wholly to the Lord. Polycarp had come to know the God who wants a person's entire life.

In a letter to the Philippian believers, after many admonishments on godly behavior, Polycarp wrote, "Let us, therefore, become imitators of his patient endurance, and if we should suffer for the sake of his name, let us glorify him. For this is the example he set for us in his own person, and this is what we have believed."[13] This kind of resolve is part of a long process of faithfulness ("eighty-six years") and revelationship ("he has done me no wrong").

We are "bought with a price" (1 Corinthians 6:20), wrote Paul, therefore our lives belong to Christ. But this is not so we can boast that we are willing to die for him. It means that we live daily in conscious dedication to his will. And if he should call us to give our lives for the kingdom, then so be it. This is the life of absolute surrender.

However, coming to a place of surrender to the Lord often requires trials and difficulties because these purge sinful tendencies and false support systems—anything that hinders our relationship with God. Through our suffering, God reveals himself, and we come to trust and obey him no matter what.

---

[13] Op. Cit., *The Letter of Polycarp to the Philippians* 8:2.

In fact, Martin Luther called affliction the best book in his library, and we should not be afraid to read from it.

After I (Cathy) found myself divorced from my first husband and no longer serving in church, I threw myself into work for a production studio in Atlanta. The worldliness rose quickly and world-weariness with it. I still maintained my distance from the worst of the worldliness, keeping up my morning devotional habit and even attending church regularly. I still served the church, leading several ministries. But I was disillusioned, disenchanted with life.

One night, I drove home in a storm, so full of despair that I wished out loud that God would make a tree fall on my car and "take me home." That's when God spoke to me. Out loud. From the passenger seat of my car. He said, "If you don't want your life, I do." (I was so startled I almost hit a tree!) Over the next several days we had a conversation on this topic—though not out loud this time. He led me to surrender a wrong relationship, a job, and a few other less significant things. Each time, I envisioned handing him the surrendered item as a "rock" for him to keep.

Thanks to prior readings of the beloved Hannah Hurnard book, *Hinds Feet On High Places*, I had a context for what was happening to

> This is where I see him best: *the face of God is best reflected in the purifying flames of absolute surrender.*

deepen my revelationship. (In the book, Jesus turns each rock surrendered by Much Afraid into a jewel for her crown.) Then God said he wanted me to give him my worst fear. But I had no idea what my worst fear was! So, I asked around. A few said losing someone. A few said dying—or being maimed and not dying. The usual suspects. Then a cousin said that her worst fear was being sent to work with the cannibals in South America. When she said that, my spirit immediately said, "If ONLY he sent me! Then I would know I was sent!" As I walked away, the Lord spoke to me saying, "Your worst fear is that you will get up on that altar and I will not care enough to accept your sacrifice."

My worst fear was that my *all* was not *enough*. (Over the years, I discovered that I was not alone in this fear. Many women believe that their all is not enough.) In revealing this to me, his grace enabled me to surrender my fear to him.

As I continue to walk with him, he enables me to surrender what he brings to my attention. As swiftly as possible, I climb upon the altar, and the fire of his presence comes to burn it away. Once I surrendered completely, the process of getting upon the altar became much easier.

This is where I see him best: *the face of God is best reflected in the purifying flames of absolute surrender.*

If we know him, we will trust him. If we trust him, we will obey him. If we obey him, we will follow him in absolute surrender through death to self. This is the abundant life to which he calls us.

Journal Prompt: Ask God if there is anything you need to give up in order to better gain him.

Download our accompanying Devotional Study Guide for FREE at Revelationship.net. It contains mindful study questions, devotional cues, and journaling prompts to help you as chronicle God's revelations to you as he pursues you for a deeper relationship.

CHAPTER THIRTEEN

REVELATIONSHIP THROUGH HISTORY

These things happened to them as examples and were written down as warnings for us, on whom the fulfillment of the ages has come.

—1 Corinthians 10:11 (NIV)

When one allows the Bible to speak without drowning it out from the noise of modern criticism, a resounding pattern emerges like music from an open window on a busy street. You can hear it faintly, but the listening ear is drawn to its melody. Before long the patterns meld together reminding us that a great conductor has led the orchestra into one melodic and harmonious sound. This is revelationship through history.

The Psalmists heard the pattern and wrote of it. "Lord, help! They cried...and he rescued them from their distress. He led them straight to safety...he satisfies the thirsty and fills the hungry with good things" (Psalm 107:6-9, NLT). "Those who are wise will take all this to heart; *they will see in our history the faithful love of the Lord*" (Psalm 107:43, NLT). For those with attentive hearts, history reveals the hand of the Conductor orchestrating events.

The Bible demonstrates this in different ways. For instance, the authors of the history of Israel not only recorded the events, but they also evaluated them in light of God's involvement. The Chronicler noted that "because" the protagonist or nation sowed rebellion against God, "therefore" they reaped his judgment.[14] The Chronicler evaluated history theologically, according to God's watchful care to keep the covenant terms.

Francis Schaeffer wrote:

> If we understand this, we understand the ebb and flow of history...When people violate the character of God, this is not only sin but stupidity. It is like rubbing your hand over a rough board and getting splinters. For it opposes what we are made to be and what the

---

[14] 1 Chronicles 10:13; 2 Chronicles 12:1-2.

universe really is. God has revealed his character, and if God's people live in accordance with his character, the conditional [covenant] blessings stand. Once we understand this, we really understand the flow of history for the Jews.[15]

God tells us himself why he orchestrates the events in the history of the Jews. He does so in one of the most memorable stories of the Old Testament—Sodom and Gomorrah—a story that is so difficult that people are stumbled by it even today:

> *"Then the Lord said, 'Shall I hide from Abraham what I am about to do? Abraham will surely become a great and powerful nation, and all nations on earth will be blessed*

---

[15] Francis A. Schaffer, *Joshua and the Flow of Biblical History* (Wheaton: Crossway Books, 2004), 138.

> *through him. For I have chosen him so that **he will direct his children** and his household after him **to keep the way of the Lord by doing what is right and just, so that the Lord may bring about for Abraham what he has promised him**.*"—Genesis 18:17-20 (NIV)

By his acts in history, God revealed many things about himself, not least of which is his faithful, covenant love toward Israel, as noted above. Indeed, God supernaturally acts in history so that generations will know what is right and just, so he may bring about what he has promised us.

We are told in Genesis 18 that after the angels and pre-incarnate Christ finished eating with Abraham, all four headed toward Sodom and Gomorrah. As they walked, the Lord revealed his plans to Abraham. It is a masterful stroke of strategy clearly meant to illustrate to Abraham and the generations to follow that, from God's perspective, the plans to destroy the two cities *and* his sharing those plans with Abraham were meant to demonstrate God's righteousness and justice. From God's perspective, the actions he takes to avenge the outcry against the grievous sins of Sodom and Gomorrah reveal him as the God of mercy, righteousness, and justice. These attributes of God are central to understanding God's revelationship in history.

> *"Then the Lord said, 'The outcry against Sodom and Gomorrah is so great and their sin so grievous that I will go down and see if what they have done is as bad as the outcry that has reached me. If not, I will know.'"* (vs. 20-21, NIV)

What kind of an environment would be rampant with sin so grievous that the outcry of those suffering—the innocent—would warrant the God of the Universe to come down to see it for himself? A holy God (in whom there is no evil) is the only one who can mete out such justice properly, weighing the balance of citizens who had already lost their lives against the innocent citizens still alive. We can comfort ourselves with the understanding that he did not take their death lightly—*as evidenced by his coming to hear for himself*—and would know their innocence or guilt, gathering the innocent to Himself in eternity.

The final reason for the destruction of Sodom and Gomorrah is revealed in God's exchanges with Abraham: when Abraham negotiates with God for the cities, God promises that if there are even ten righteous, he will spare the cities.

A cursory reading might lead us to believe that Abraham changed God's mind or at least influenced it. However, we know that God does not change—he is immutable. He declares his immutability many different times in many ways throughout the Bible. The exchange between Abraham and God as he negotiates does not reveal God changing—indeed, he destroys both cities. It does not even reveal God "relenting" or being influenced—*he destroys both cities.*

When the angels practically drag both Lot and his family from the city so they can escape, we find out the truth and what God knew all along: there was only one righteous man in the city—and he was removed.

In a sense, Sodom and Gomorrah were already wrecked. The only answer to cleanse the world of the grievous suffering they had perpetrated on others was destruction. As in the case of the Great Flood, a holy God had contended with them long enough.

What does this entire exchange and the destruction of Sodom and Gomorrah reveal about God? It must be something more than just the destruction of two cities for their sins—God will do that many more times to come, with or without an announcement. It must be something more than the cries of the innocent who need justice. It must be something more than the completion of the cup of wrath from which the cities' inhabitants drink to the dregs—this too will happen again and again until the end of time.

The story of Sodom and Gomorrah (and quite frankly the revelation behind all that God does in history) is found in these same verses. There is a contingency clause in the statement: "so that the Lord may bring about for Abraham what he has promised." Perhaps it's not so much a contingency clause but more of a dependency clause: if Abraham and his descendants do what is right and just, God *will be able to* give all that is promised.

Just as Abraham is singularly focused on a long-awaited son, God is focused on the coming of his own Son. This is the promise of a savior that he gave Adam and Eve and each righteous person after them. The "what" that God promised Abraham was not just a son or a lineage that lives on, it was the One who would reunite heaven and earth and rescue us from willful rebellion and our rogue state. The whole Bible is woven with this promise because he wants to be our God, for us to be his people, and for him to dwell in our midst.

This Tripartite Promise was never *just* for the Jews—it was always so that all nations and all peoples would be "blessed" by restoration to our relationship with God prior to the fall. It is the Jews, however, whom he chose to set apart, calling them to holiness again and again, so he *could* bring a Savior through them.

The reason God had to bring justice to Sodom and Gomorrah by destroying it, was so that Abraham's generations would come to know the ways of the Lord, so he could have a people of his own—holy and set apart. He did this not because he had given up on the rest of the world but so that he could send a Savior and thus *rescue* the entire world from its rebellion and reunite it with heaven, just as it was in the Garden of Eden.

> Ultimately, God entered history to reveal himself not just by a theophany, as he did to Abraham, but by actual incarnation. Jesus was born as a child, grew and matured, suffered and died—and was resurrected. By doing so, God revealed his glory (John 1:14) in the greatest act of revelationship in history.

We find this again when God delivered Israel out of bondage in Egypt, leading the nation into their Promised Land. God was working with other "Gentile" nations in similar ways as well. "Did I not bring Israel up from Egypt," the prophet Amos observed, "the Philistines from Caphtor and the Arameans from Kir?" (Amos 9:7, NIV). The Bible unequivocally recognizes the involvement of God in historical events beyond the boundaries of Israel. This is also clearly revealed in the book of Jonah.

When we move to the New Testament, we see that God had already prepared the "soil" of the Mediterranean world for the gospel. Through the spread of Hellenism under Alexander the Great, the Greek language was spoken as a second language, allowing immediate communication among most people groups. Because of the diaspora of the Jews, there were synagogues in most major metropolises, providing an immediate platform for sharing the gospel. And due to the Pax Romana, there was a certain safety in place for travelers and well-engineered roads and established shipping lanes as well.[16] This doesn't mean that the spread of Christianity didn't face great challenges—it most certainly did—but the soil was long prepared.

Further, if God foreknows the future, as he demonstrated with Sodom and Gomorrah, then it's not unreasonable that he may choose to reveal it ahead of time. The skeptic can devise elaborate explanations to deny the providence of God. Still, it's hard to explain how many of the predictions were beyond the lifetimes of the prophets (such as the Messianic prophecies) or out of the control of those they involved (such as prophecies fulfilled during the passion of Christ). Is Bible history a series of random events? Or was God directing things according to his plan? The answer might have resided in the opinion of the reader, except for these prophecies.

---

[16] H. I. Hester, *The Heart of the New Testament* (Liberty, MO: Quality Press, 1963), 49.

Ultimately, God entered history to reveal himself not just by a theophany, as he did to Abraham, but by actual incarnation. Jesus was born as a child, grew and matured, ministered, suffered, and died—and was resurrected. Through this incarnation, God revealed his glory (John 1:14) in the greatest act of revelationship in history.

Can we not see the love of God thus revealed in history? Can we not see the power of heaven invading this age by Christ's resurrection? Since Jesus was resurrected, then it follows that there will be a future resurrection for all those in him. The one inaugurated the other.

Further, the judgment event that began at Christ's resurrection guarantees that the future, final judgment will take place. History has a goal where sin and death meet their end (1 Corinthians 15:15-28). Therefore, history is moving toward a special "Day of the Lord" where everything will be put right, and God's righteous character will be revealed in history.

Journal Prompt: How did God interrupt history to deal with revelationship? How has he interrupted your story?

Download our accompanying Devotional Study Guide for FREE at Revelationship.net. It contains mindful study questions, devotional cues, and journaling prompts to help you as chronicle God's revelations to you as he pursues you for a deeper relationship.

CHAPTER FOURTEEN

REVELATIONSHIP THROUGH CHURCH

Come and be his 'living stones' who are continually being assembled into a sanctuary for God. For now you serve as holy priests, offering up spiritual sacrifices that he readily accepts through Jesus Christ.

—1 Peter 2:5 (TPT)

When believers gather in his name, Christ promises to be among them (Matthew 18:20). In other words, when Christians gather as a church, the opportunity for revelationship exists because Christ's presence uniquely dwells there. A church exists not just as a gathering of like-minded followers of Christ but as the dwelling place of his presence. His promise to be among us is not a side note or a pleasant word to encourage the disciples. It forms the basis of what it means to be a church. He desires to make himself manifest in and through the gathering. Therefore, a church should be, first and foremost, *presence-based*.

The apostle Peter referred to members of this Church as "living stones" (1 Peter 2:1-12, NIV) set in, alongside others, in a spiritual temple for the presence of God. The purpose of a temple, of course, is to house the presence of God among humankind. Thus, a Church is called to manifest the presence of God and bring him glory.

The apostle Paul described this gathering as the Body of Christ (1 Corinthians 12:27), where we need the contribution of one another's gifts to mature spiritually (Ephesians 4:11-13). "When you come together," Paul wrote, "everyone has a hymn, or a word of instruction, a revelation, a tongue or an interpretation. All of these must be done for the strengthening of the church" (1 Corinthians 14:26, NIV). A church provides revelationship through corporate fellowship and the varied contributions of its many members, which, in turn, builds up everyone's faith.

It is at this church where leaders preach the Word of God, introduce us to the beliefs of Christianity, and teach us what it means to love the Lord and serve one another. It is where the precious gifts of the Spirit operate through the many members and by which the Lord communicates with us what is on his heart.

Ch. 14: Revelationship through Church

It is where we can worship the Lord in harmony with one another, brought to the very throne of God.

In fact, when a church gathers together, the Lord may impart a gift (charisma) to a believer through the laying on of hands. Paul describes this in 1 Timothy 4:14 in which he reminds Timothy to not neglect the gift given to him through a prophecy of the elders. Likewise, a church's prophets judge the expressions of the gifts (1 Corinthians 14:29) during the meetings. Thus, a church becomes both an important place for imparting the means of revelationship as well as the proving ground for that revelationship.

Together we share the body and blood of Christ at the Lord's Table, experiencing his presence as we solemnly partake. We do this in remembrance of Christ (revelationship), and we do this together. (Indeed, Christianity was never meant to be just a personal thing.) We are meant to celebrate his presence with one another, even as Jesus did with the disciples.

Together we witness the baptism of believers. This public "object lesson" demonstrates to the world the candidate's willingness to follow Christ in his death, burial, and resurrection. Here, also, is revelationship expressed in community.

Communion and water baptism were never meant to be merely form and ritual. Communion not only proclaims the Lord's death (1 Corinthians 11:26), but also requires us to examine ourselves "to recognize the body of our Lord" (1 Corinthians 11:29, NIV) in revelationship. He is vitally among us. Similarly, water baptism illustrates outwardly what takes place inwardly. We have died to sin, buried the old nature, and now live for Christ Jesus (Romans 6:1-14). When we come up out of the waters of baptism, we demonstrate our renewed desire to offer ourselves continually to him.

A church can certainly reject Christ's manifest presence and become religious–cold and lifeless. But

Christ evaluates the heart condition of each local church (as in Revelation 2-3). He knocks at the door of a lukewarm church and offers close fellowship to those who let him in. Even at similar church gatherings today, when someone testifies about their repentance, this may motivate others to repent. Soon the congregation praises God and his presence falls on the congregants afresh. In this way, a corporate response of repentance brings about revelationship.

Once, in the church in which I (Cathy) grew up in Atlanta, a bit of the worldwide outpouring of gold dust as a sign and wonder showed up in services for a few months. A young Sunday school student of mine told me in a heartbroken voice that she didn't have gold dust on her hands and didn't understand why. I told her, "Put your hands together, we'll pray, and it will be there." I don't recall the words I used out loud, but my heart was desperately crying out: "Oh God! You must answer her NOW!" She opened her hands, and they were covered in the shimmering dust. Another time, my children's choir was talking with me about having faith for things we ask for in prayer. I was not well-trained in prayer yet, but I think I was clear that faith was the necessary ingredient (James 1). They asked if they could pray for snow on Christmas Eve when we performed our special songs. I agreed, but I told them sternly they must believe and not doubt.

It snowed, of course, on Christmas Eve, as we sang Christmas carols to welcome the families into the warm vestibule. The kids' faces were shining with revelation: God answered their prayers!

The Church also offers this revelationship to the world. Indeed, the very mission of the Church is to reveal Christ to the world (Mt.28:19-20) and establish his Kingdom. The Church reveals the meek and lowly lamb of God (the image of Christ revealed in the gospel) who takes away the sins of the world (the power of the gospel). This is why our mission as Christians requires that we—the ones with actual hands, feet, and mouths—go into all the world and preach the gospel of Christ. By doing so, we invite the world to partner in this revelationship.

Unfortunately, the display of Christ's image and the power of the gospel have become so obscured that unbelievers no longer see the relevance of the Church (of America, in particular) because the world no longer sees Christ revealed through it. Christ described this as salt that had lost its flavor (Matthew 5:13).

Revelation of the gospel—who Christ is and what he does—is no longer a key element in the Western Church today. R. C. Sproul said that he'd ask his seminary students, many of whom were pastors, to concisely state what the gospel is, *he was delighted when even 10% could.*

Many have written books, seminars, and sermons bemoaning the loss of the Church's saltiness. They focus on everything from lack of prayer to lack of worship or people no longer being the hands and feet of Christ. Some have even written the Church off for the lack of God's presence. But John tells us in Revelation the culprit is that we have forgotten our first love and have stopped doing what we did when we first came to Christ.

To respond to Christ's call to return to our first love, we must understand and walk in the gospel with a full understanding of what Christ did when his Kingdom broke in, what he is doing now, and what he will do in the future. It is necessary to preach the gospel so that we can appropriate the Kingdom of Heaven into the now. If we cannot do this, we cannot expect to live in equality, rest, joy, and righteousness—all of which is provided by the humble message of Christ's gospel.

Ch. 14: Revelationship through Church

The gospel is the antidote to the tyranny of pride and self in this world. The humility the gospel brings—the understanding of our right position before God—is the sacred perfume revealed through lives displaying Christ, rousing the senses of those dying in fear and trapped in sin. Such is the revelationship of the Church that "inherits the earth."

Journal Prompt: How do the ordinances (sacraments) of the Church bring revelationship?

Download our accompanying Devotional Study Guide for FREE at Revelationship.net. It contains mindful study questions, devotional cues, and journaling prompts to help you as chronicle God's revelations to you as he pursues you for a deeper relationship.

CHAPTER FIFTEEN

A LIFETIME OF REVELATIONSHIP

Long ago, at many times and in many ways, God spoke to our fathers by the prophets, but in these last days he has spoken to us by his Son, whom he appointed the heir of all things, through whom also he created the world.

—Hebrew 1:1-2 (ESV)

If anyone illustrated a lifetime of encountering God, it would be my (Randy's) mother (Cathy's grandmother). God always seemed to be speaking to her. In fact, after she recently passed away, and while carefully cleaning out her things, I found a stack of devotional journals full of prophetic words—some for herself, but most for others. Prophecy consists of hearing and saying what is on the heart of God—and my mother was good at listening to God's heart.

On one occasion, mother was given a prophetic word for a long-time friend regarding her husband. He had been struggling with cancer and was scheduled for surgery the next day. The word contained specific guidance for the couple to pray. They received it and prayed that night. The next day when her husband had surgery, no cancer was found! And God added another nineteen years to his life.

When my mother worked at the Christian Broadcasting Network (CBN), Pat Robertson recognized her gift and allowed her to speak prophetically to the CBN staff. Even when well-known guests would visit CBN, mother was permitted to prophesy to them. She once prophesied to Lt. Colonel Oliver North, a well-known Marine who worked for the National Security Administration during the Reagan years.

On one occasion mother had a prophetic word for Pat Robertson. The word was that he had two "bodyguards" named "integrity" and "uprightness." They would guard him, but the Bible would keep him. (We think that's solid advice for any minister!)

The first time my mother visited CBN in Virginia Beach, she reached up to touch the door handle and when she did, she felt as though electricity surged through her. The Lord immediately spoke to her, "You will go through these doors many days." Through her phone work at CBN, she led thousands to salvation and into the Baptism of the Holy Spirit. In fact, she had a particularly strong anointing for ministering Spirit Baptism with the evidence of speaking in tongues—a supernatural event that opens the door to deeper revelationship.

One particularly interesting way God spoke to her was by giving her a single, keyword—often a word she did not know. She would have to look the word up in her dictionary, and then God would begin to communicate what was on his heart.

Psalm 91:4 states, "He will cover you with his feathers, and under his wings you will find refuge" (NIV). This was one of Mother's favorite verses because she used to find feathers from time to time—in her jewelry box or silverware drawer or in her luggage, especially when she traveled to the Ruth Heflin camp meetings. These gave her assurance that God's angels were always present, working on her behalf.

One time, Mother was traveling with a prophetess from the Seattle area, who was reading from Isaiah as Mother drove. Suddenly, they began driving through a cloud of feathers that flew all around the car. This lasted for about two miles, but no other vehicle was in sight.

I (Cathy) have inherited feather-related revelations. Once, my younger sister visited my husband and me when we lived in Valdosta, Georgia. I lent her my new earrings to go with her cute outfit. Somewhere between Valdosta and our tour of Thomasville, Georgia, she lost one of my new earrings. Small thing, of course, but something I cared about. So, when we returned home, I shooed everyone into the house and said I was going to walk a bit outside and pray about my earring. I closed the door, stood on the steps, and simply asked God to return my earring to me.

I walked toward the car (thinking to check the inside of the car), and not more than half a dozen steps away lay my earring—just at the edge of the brick path—lying next to a grey feather. Make of it what you will, but that has led me to build up, over time, a rather large reservoir of faith when it comes to lost things—mostly because I lose things. Often.

I pray and God returns lost items to me or brings to my mind an exact picture of where they are. Just last week I found one of my diamond earrings embedded in the carpet (I didn't know it was even lost). When I couldn't find the mate, I spent twenty minutes scouring the carpet nearby with a flashlight and fussing at myself. Then, I stood up, took a breath, and prayed. I no sooner said, "Amen," than my foot stepped on the other one, in the very spot I had combed earlier.

My husband, who never loses anything, just shakes his head, and assures me that it's God's way of showing me his careful, special love for me. It's a revelation of the God who cares even for the tiniest of things and listens to me when I pray. I've already passed on both lessons to my children who now know the first response to losing things is to pray. (The second is to go clean one's room!)

I (Randy) remember recently talking to a young man who, unfortunately, had deconstructed his faith and had become an atheist—something that is a condition growing among his generation. This young man had arrived at his position partly because of bitterness toward the Church. But after all his arguments for why God does not exist, I simply asked, "But what about the angels that have appeared to my mother?" He didn't have much more to say after that. Mother's simple faith and God's daily presence in her life demolished all his arguments against truth.

"God is there, and he is not silent." He has revealed himself in the designs of the universe and in the sophistication of the smallest parts of life—our DNA. When we have a relationship with him through his Son, Jesus Christ, the Spirit opens our eyes to his revelation all around us—and he speaks to us personally—individually—even quietly, as he did with Mother.

You cannot know God in any intimate way without first having a relationship with him—a covenantal, biblical relationship. In John 16:14-15, Jesus states that the Holy Spirit will "bring glory to me by taking from what is mine and making it known to you. All that belongs to the Father is mine. That is why I said the Spirit will take from what is mine and make it known to you." The Holy Spirit can bring a lifetime of revelationship. We only need to ask in faith.

Download our accompanying Devotional Study Guide for FREE at Revelationship.net. It contains mindful study questions, devotional cues, and journaling prompts to help you as chronicle God's revelations to you as he pursues you for a deeper relationship.

A FINAL WORD

Responding in Revelationship

What other God has descended for relationship? No idol or god does so—only the Living God. Which brings us to another question: How should we respond to this God who condescends to us?

It is the "coming near" that gets me every time. He is under no obligation to come, yet he does. WHY? Why does our God draw near? He draws near because of his grace and his desire to make himself known, for the purpose of revelationship.

For Job, God comes to answer the charges Job hurls to the sky. God comes. God doesn't answer Job's charges directly and he certainly doesn't have to answer them at all (which is the point of the "guided tour" God takes Job on at the end of the book), but he does come. He comes in the storm and Job is made fully and completely aware of the dreadfulness of being in the presence of the Living God.

John's revelation is the most intense and complete. The first revelation of Christ among the lampstands prompts John to fall dead—which seems to be a common response to the holiness of God. Then in chapter four, John is strengthened, taken up by the Holy Spirit through the doorway of Heaven, and commissioned to write and tell the world of what he has seen of the revelation of Jesus Christ:

"I am the First and the Last. I am the Living One; I was dead, and now look, I am alive for ever and ever! And I hold the keys of death and Hades." (Revelation 1:17b-18, NIV)

What awaits us when we ascend God's holy hill? What awaits us when God descends? He is a God who descends to us for the purpose of revelationship. May we, by God's grace, ascend.

FREE DOWNLOAD!

DEVOTIONAL GUIDE & WORKBOOK

REVELATIONSHIP.NET

Coming

Soon!

REVELATIONSHIP.NET

MORE BOOKS BY DR. RANDY COLVER

Sustaining the Fires of Revival
Turning God's Visitation Into A Habitation

by Dr. Randy Colver
forward by Pastor Steve Gray

REVELATIONSHIP.NET

REVELATIONSHIP.NET

THE COURTROOM MINISTRY of HEAVEN

A Journey into the Celestial Courtroom Procedures of Heaven

MORE BOOKS BY DR. RANDY COLVER